TRADITIONAL ENGLISH GR

D0621988

D9A

Related Macmillan titles:

SHAKESPEARE'S LANGUAGE: AN INTRODUCTION
N. F. Blake

A GUIDE TO CHAUCER'S LANGUAGE
David Burnley

SEMIOTICS AND THE PHILOSOPHY OF LANGUAGE
Umberto Eco

VARIETIES OF ENGLISH
Dennis Freeborn

A COURSE BOOK IN ENGLISH GRAMMAR
Dennis Freeborn

LITERARY LANGUAGE FROM CHAUCER TO
JOHNSON
A. J. Gilbert

THE DICTIONARY OF EVEN MORE DISEASED
ENGLISH
Kenneth Hudson

THE LANGUAGE OF THE TEENAGE REVOLUTION
Kenneth Hudson

ENGLISH GRAMMAR FOR TODAY
A New Introduction
Geoffrey Leech, Margaret Deuchar and Robert Hoogenraad

A DICTIONARY OF GOOD ENGLISH
A Guide to Current Usage
S. G. McKaskill

TRADITIONAL ENGLISH GRAMMAR AND BEYOND

N. F. BLAKE

MACMILLAN

First published 1988

Published by
Higher and Further Education Division
MACMILLAN PUBLISHERS LTD
Houndmills, Basingstoke, Hampshire RG21 2XS
and London
Companies and representatives
throughout the world

Typeset by Wessex Typesetters
(Division of The Eastern Press Ltd)
Frome, Somerset

Printed in Hong Kong

British Library Cataloguing in Publication Data
Blake, N. F.
Traditional English grammar and beyond.
1. English language—Grammar—1950–
I. Title
428.2   PE1112
ISBN 0–333–39920–X
ISBN 0–333–39921–8 Pbk

Contents

For Dorinda Jane

Preface

There are many reasons why you should want to pick up a book which has *Grammar* in its title, and those reasons are so diverse that it is not possible for a single book to satisfy them all. So I need to offer a brief explanation as to why I have written this particular grammar. The study of English grammar has proceeded in the following two ways recently. Modern linguists have been obsessed with the theoretical problems of language and so have proposed new theoretical methodologies for analysing language. These have sometimes spawned grammars, which are difficult for those with no linguistic background to follow since such readers do not understand some of the preconceptions which lie behind them. On the other hand, full descriptions of English have been written such as the one by Professor Quirk and his colleagues. These often have a somewhat eclectic methodology, for they use not only traditional terminology but also some more modern terms. Those who come new to the study of the English language find both approaches rather daunting, because they have been taught neither. It is clear that there is room for an introduction to the study of English grammar which starts with traditional approaches and then incorporates some of the newer terms from modern linguistics. The new A level English Language papers established by the Joint Matriculation Board (Manchester) and the University of London Examinations Board provide a good example of this need. This book has been written with this kind of need in mind. Readers who find it helpful, but who feel modification might make the book even more useful, are invited to write to me with their suggestions.

I am indebted to my colleagues and to my students in the

Department of English Language at Sheffield University for their ideas and support with this volume. I am also grateful to many of the participants at conferences we have organised on the JMB A level English Language course for their comments, which have often helped me in deciding what to include and how to put it. I am particularly grateful to Sandra Burton, who has once again produced such excellent copy for the publishers.

NFB

Introduction

'They was watching the telly.' If in a novel you came across a character who spoke like this, you are likely to make certain assumptions about his social standing, because the sentence will be interpreted as an example of incorrect English or, if you prefer, of bad grammar. In what is usually described as 'good English' *they*, which is a plural subject, should be followed by the plural verb *were*; the occurrence of the singular verb *was* with the plural *they* is characteristic of non-standard speakers of English only. All languages exhibit similar variations in usage which have arisen from social and regional factors, and usually one of the variant forms is singled out as the accepted usage for literary and other purposes. This form then gains social prestige at the expense of other varieties. In England this variety, often referred to as standard English or as the Queen's English, is associated with educational attainment, and that is why speakers who do not conform to this variety in their usage run the risk of being considered poorly educated. In some cases people who fail to observe this standard may find that it affects their career prospects, for some employers still take the view that they should not employ a person who, in their opinion, cannot speak or write properly.

The interpretation of what constitutes good or bad English usually follows certain rules which are associated with traditional grammar. This is the methodology and approach to language whose origins can be traced back to the classical period and which was almost universally taught in England until well into the twentieth century. It has often been abandoned in schools today because of the onset of what is known as modern linguistics, or what are simply more recent methodologies of grammatical investigation, for modern linguists have always regarded traditional grammar as old-fashioned and lacking in theoretical rigour. The advantages which are sometimes claimed for modern linguistics are that its approaches are descriptive rather than prescriptive, they are more coherent and consistent, and they pay greater attention to all varieties of a language rather than to just the standard form. Whether these claims can be justified or not, they have led many people to assume that traditional grammar is inappropriate today and so should be avoided. In practice it has meant that teachers of English in schools have been unwilling to teach traditional grammar lest they should be considered out of touch with recent fashion. At the same time many teachers remain unfamiliar with the methodologies of modern linguistics, and so they end up by not teaching any form of grammar at all to their pupils. Hence it is not unusual for students today to arrive at university with only a sketchy knowledge of any grammatical approach to language. If they do have some familiarity with a grammatical methodology it is more likely to be that of traditional grammar which they have picked up from learning a foreign language rather than from being taught it as part of English.

It is worth considering in more detail some of the charges which have been levelled against traditional grammar. The best-known one is that it is prescriptive – that is, it contains rules for what is correct or incorrect in the language and it lays down rules of usage which speakers of the language must follow. Today it is thought that grammars ought to be only descriptive – that is, they should describe what is the usage in the language by analysing what is spoken or written, and they should not posit rules for usage. Furthermore it is usually held against traditional grammar that its prescriptivism is based on the individual grammarian's prejudices or on the foundations of Latin grammar; and neither is considered appropriate for English. It can never be justified, it is suggested, to lay down rules for one language on the basis of what happens in a different language or of an individual's own whims. Thus, for example, it was a familiar assertion in older grammars of English that *It is me* is incorrect; one should use *It is I.* The reason for this is that in Latin the verb *to be* had the same case after it as before it. Since in this case *it* is a subject, the verb *is* (which is a part of the verb *to be*) ought to be followed by a word which could act as a subject.* Since we cannot say in English *Me am coming*, but only *I am coming*, it was concluded from this reasoning we should say *It is I* and not *It is me* because *I* is the subject form. This proposition about the correctness of *It is I* was made on the basis of Latin grammar, on the assumption that the logic of that language could be applied to English. If it were so applied, it was assumed that English would become a more expressive and correct language. However, this rule was made without reference to what had actually happened in English in the past and what is the normal usage at present. It is hardly surprising, therefore, that this particular rule never won total acceptance among the speakers of the language; it is now largely ignored.

Two points may be made in connection with this example. The first is that the rules derived from traditional grammar have normally been applied only to the written language, and not to the spoken language, though there has naturally been some influence from the former on the latter. But the phrase *It is me* or rather *It's me* is one which is more characteristic of the spoken language, since there are few situations in which one might expect to find this expression in written varieties of English. Hence it is hardly surprising that in this particular example the recommendations of the traditional grammarians have had little impact. The second is that this rule has nothing in itself to do with traditional grammar as a particular approach to analysing language. Traditional grammar is a method by which it is possible to break the language down into smaller parts so that the make-up of the language can be studied. As a methodology it need not involve the promulgation of the rules of good English. Any methodology, whether traditional grammar or modern linguistics, can be used as the basis for providing rules which speakers of that language are advised to follow. The methodology of traditional grammar as such cannot be

---

* These terms are explained later in the book. If you are unfamiliar with them, please consult the index to find out where they are treated.

criticised simply because some grammarians have used it as the basis for their rules for standard grammar. It would be perfectly feasible to write a descriptive account of modern English using the terminology of traditional grammar. Indeed, descriptions of both modern English and of older varieties of English have been constructed using this methodology. Prescriptivism is not inherent in traditional grammar even if it has frequently been associated with it. We cannot jettison the grammar simply because some people have used it for particular ends of which we disapprove.

Because of its reliance on Latin and its primary involvement with the written variety of English, it may well be that traditional grammar has been discarded by some because it is considered too elitist. This may be so, and the advent of modern linguistics has directed attention to other varieties of English such as regional and social dialects which have less prestige, and it has meant that these varieties have been accorded fuller attention and respect as complete systems of communication. However, one must add that there is nothing in traditional grammar which would prevent it from being used as the methodology to investigate these varieties. Quite apart from that, one may also question whether the modern interest in spoken language and dialects should inhibit the investigation of the written language, by which we may understand the standard language. So much of the language which we use is in a written form, to say nothing of the whole range of English literature, for which some kind of grammatical methodology is needed. It may well be, as is usually stated, that speech is the primary form of communication and that writing is developed from it; but that should not prevent full attention from being given to the written form. Students analysing literature need some guidance as to which type of language to employ as does anyone who writes; and that means having some methodology which can be used to provide the necessary framework for the grammatical discussion.

The claim that traditional grammar has been based too exclusively on prescriptive attitudes to the language has been pushed too far. There is after all not as much difference as is often implied between prescriptive and descriptive approaches to language. A dictionary such as *The Oxford English Dictionary* may have been compiled descriptively by reading as many texts as possible and by recording the words found in them. It will thus include a descriptive list of the words in the language or at least of those words found by the readers. Yet, in questions of pronunciation and meaning, there may well be more than an element of indicating what is right rather than what is an accurate description, since the editor will have to exercise his subjective judgement in these matters. Others may not agree with his statements. As soon as the dictionary is published many readers will treat it as prescriptive and will not accept as permissible usage words which are not included in the dictionary. In the same way a grammar may be based on an analysis of a corpus of material which may be either written or spoken, or indeed both. This analysis may be rigorously descriptive in intention, though many of its users will assume that the description enshrines rules of English usage which they should follow, because that is what most users expect from a grammar. Many modern grammars are not, in any case, as objective as modern linguists like to pretend, for the corpus of material on which they base their analysis may not contain examples of everything they want. They may have to make statements without any evidence for them. They also place an asterisk against those expressions which they consider unacceptable in English. This asterisk fulfils the same function as those rules which state that certain constructions are incorrect. This practice inevitably sets up the expectation that some things are correct and others incorrect, and it also raises the question of what basis there is for claiming that a particular utterance is incorrect and so deserves an asterisk. Often the reason is either that a given form does not occur in the corpus of material or that the grammarian accepts intuitively that the usage is incorrect. Even if a form which the grammarian regards as incorrect occurs in the material he is using, he may still mark it with an asterisk and treat it as a mistake on the part of the speaker or writer. In other words, where traditional grammarians used Latin or logic to support their claims, modern linguists use their intuition. It is not self-evident that the one is more reliable than the other.

It may well be that some element of prescriptivism is inevitable in discussions of language, and we deceive ourselves if we pretend otherwise. This applies particularly to the standard language, since that is an artificial written language which can hardly be said to spring directly from any spoken variety. It has developed through the efforts of grammarians who have tried to standardise the usage of this particular variety. Although many speakers may think they model their speech on the written standard, in practice this is rarely the case; equally the written language is not based on the speech habits of these people. Because the standard language is an artificial construct, it needs some rules for its regulation and guidance; and there may well be an element of arbitrariness in such rules. Provided they do not diverge too abruptly from the spoken usage of educated people, they are likely to be observed. Nevertheless, the rules are not likely to be based on current speech habits, for the standard written language is inevitably somewhat conservative.

Although some elements of prescription may be inevitable in discussions of language, it is sensible to keep the question of prescription quite separate from the methodology employed in a grammar. It is to the rationale of traditional grammar that we must now turn. Language is composed of small segments which are joined together to form larger units, and these units in their turn unite to form even bigger units. We can arrange the units of language in an ascending order of sounds, syllables, words, phrases, clauses and sentences. A unit higher up this order consists of one or more of the immediately preceding unit; for example, a syllable will contain one or more sounds, a word one or more syllables. It might be possible to construct a grammar using any of these units as the starting-point, though not all are likely to be equally successful. Traditional grammar works on the basis of words, and is to that extent a word-based grammar. In this it differs from many modern grammars which tend to start with a larger unit such as the sentence, and are thus sentence-based grammars. With a word-based grammar, words are considered the primary units and larger units are made by joining them together. In a sentence-based grammar, the primary unit is the sentence and that is then broken down into its constituent parts to provide the smaller units. A considerable difference in attitude is embodied in these apparently rather trivial differences. In a sentence-based grammar the smaller units will simply be regarded as functional parts of the sentence which have in themselves little independence or inherent meaning apart from their role in the sentence. In a word-based grammar the word is given the greatest importance, and how and what it means a primary function. The sentence may often seem to be little more than a string of words.

Words are not the smallest of the units in a sentence, but they are the ones most easily recognised by speakers of English. At least in the written form of the language, words have a space both before and after them. In addition the average person is perfectly familiar with words because they are the elements of the language which are collected in dictionaries. Although it might be difficult to find a definition of what a word is which embraced all the words in a language, they nevertheless represent the unit which most people are familiar with and find easy to handle. Even so, there are some problems with recognising what are words. Although written as single words, many people assume that *won't* and *shan't* are two words because they stand for *will not* and *shall not*. In fact forms such as *won't* and *shan't* are usually discouraged in formal written language, although they are found in informal style. It might be simplest to assume that where these spellings occur they are single words as the spelling implies, for it is perfectly possible to add a negative element to a word and let it remain a single word. Thus we are quite content to accept *human* and *inhuman* as words, though the latter is the negative of the former, and the same may also be understood to apply to *shall* and *shan't*. More of a problem occurs when two or three words together form a single concept. Sometimes such words are hyphenated to make them into a word and sometimes they remain as distinct words. Thus *mother-in-law* could be treated as a single word, but its plural form *mothers-in-law* suggests that really the words are meant to be taken separately, since it is the first rather than the last element which has the plural *-s* ending attached to it. In the possessive form, however, we say *the mother-in-law's attitude*, where the *'s* ending (which is the indicator of the possessive) comes at the end of the word rather than at the end of its first element. It is not *the mother's-in-law attitude*. The same applies to groups of words which are not currently hyphenated together. Although we do not hyphenate *Queen of England*, we do put the *'s* indicating the possessive after *England* rather than after *Queen*. So we say *the Queen of England's corgis* rather than *the Queen's of England corgis*. However, the plural acts differently, for in that case we say *the Queens of England have corgis* rather than *the Queen of Englands have corgis*. There is some uncertainty among the speakers of the language about such forms, for the plural suggests that we are dealing with three independent words but the possessive suggests that the three words are treated as a single unit. Although we must accept that these ambiguous examples occur, for the most part the division of English into its constituent words is not likely to cause many problems. If necessary one can always consult a dictionary to get a decision on what constitutes a word.

The principle of a word-based grammar is that words form the important constituents of a language which are joined together to form the larger units. It also accepts that the words in a language can be divided into various classes. This is because each class of word has a different kind of meaning and so has a separate function in larger groupings such as sentences. In a sentence such as *The boy assumed she was dead*, one can see that certain words fill roles which could not be occupied by the other word classes. Thus *assumed* could not be put after *the* to give either *the assume* or *the assumed*. Similarly *boy* could not occupy the slot filled by *assumed*, for there is no form *boyed* in English. The same is true of *dead*, which does not have the form *deaded*, though in this case it could occupy the position after *the* to give *the dead*. *Was* is like *assumed*, for it is not possible to have *the was*. The words which make up the English language can be said to fall into different categories. Usually nine categories are said to be characteristic of English, and these are nouns, verbs, pronouns, adjectives, adverbs, conjunctions, prepositions, articles and interjections. The meanings of these various types will be explained in Chapter 1, but it should be said now that the names of these classes are all based on Latin forms because the development of traditional grammar has been based on Latin grammar. However, the meanings they had in the parent language may not necessarily be appropriate to their meaning in English. This is a matter which will be taken up in more detail later.

When the grammar being used is word-based, it is helpful if one can decide from the word itself into which category it fits. This is not usually possible in English because some words may occupy more than one function, as we saw was true of *dead* in the last paragraph. In some languages such variation is either impossible or very difficult, because words indicate their function through specific endings, and the endings inhibit, if not prevent, the use of a word in more than one function. But in English a word such as *round* can be introduced into sentences in which it will occupy clearly separate functions. Consider for example

1 They sang a round.
2 They played with a round ball.
3 The boat rounded the Cape yesterday.
4 They lived round the corner.
5 Come round to my house tonight.

In each of these sentences *round* plays a different role from that in any of the others. It is for this reason that many modern linguists have abandoned traditional grammar, for they say that in theory at least any word in English can be used in any function. English is in that respect a free language, and as such the use of a word-based methodology is inappropriate, even if it may be suitable for other languages. It is inappropriate because it ought to be possible to tell from the form of a word what function it has in a sentence. While this may be true of Latin, it need not follow that a similar type of word-grammar is inappropriate to English. For, although it may be theoretically possible for any word in English to be used in any function, in practice this is not the case. We do think of many words as falling into precise categories, and for the most part the freedom to use words in other functions is not exploited as fully as the theoretical position implies. This may be made clearer by considering a couple of examples.

Think, for example, of the word *cafeteria*. We all know what it means. It is a type of café where one takes a tray and chooses a meal for oneself from among the dishes which are displayed on the counter. By the time one reaches the end of the counter one has acquired all that one wants to eat and drink, and everything is paid for before the customer starts to eat anything. To anyone familiar with traditional grammar the word *cafeteria* is a noun. It is true that in English there is nothing in the form of this word which makes it part of the noun class rather than any other word class. In theory it would be possible to construct sentences in which it was used as a different word class, as in

1   Will you cafeteria with me today?
2   It's only a cafeteria joint.

Both these sentences are likely to seem strange to the average speaker of English, the first particularly so. It presumably means something like 'Will you join me for a meal in the cafeteria today?' The other sentence may appear less foreign, and would mean 'It's a café which operates self-service rather than waitress-service meals.' The important point is that we do regard these sentences as aberrant, because we think of *cafeteria* as a noun and not as any other word class. Its use in sentences such as those given is likely to be considered either poetic or humorous; they are not part of normal usage.

This being so, it is in poetic language that traditional grammar can be far more helpful to the critic than some modern forms of grammatical analysis. In a sentence-based grammar each sentence is broken down into its constituent parts, and each part has no meaning in its own right but is only a functional element within the larger whole. A word is not specifically a noun or a verb, but merely an element of a sentence which is acting in the role of subject or predicator or whatsoever. But poets rely upon their readers making a response to their language which involves them in responding to the nature of particular words. For example, in *Antony and Cleopatra* Antony says of his following 'The hearts/That spaniel'd me at heels' (iv.xii.20–1). In a modern grammar which is sentence-based one would simply say that *spaniel'd* was fulfilling a verbal function and was in principle no different in kind from any other word which could fill the same slot in that same sentence as far as its construction was concerned. In traditional grammar one could not avoid labelling *spaniel* a noun, which is indeed how we all think of the word. If you asked someone to what class of word *spaniel* belonged without providing any context, there would be no hesitation in the reply. It is a noun. Shakespeare has, however, transferred it from the noun category to the verb category. It is an example of what is sometimes called functional shift, because the word is shifted from one function (a noun) to a different one (a verb). Indeed, the concept of functional shift would be meaningless unless we thought words belonged naturally to particular classes. In using *spaniel* as a verb, Shakespeare is making his language more concrete and metaphorical. If we think of *spaniel* simply as a unit fulfilling the function of predicator in a sentence, the richness and inventiveness of Shakespeare's language are immeasurably reduced. It is only with a word-based grammar such as traditional grammar that one can appreciate Shakespeare's artistry to the full in this respect.

There can be little doubt that words have always exercised a particular fascination for writers of all kinds, and for the reader to respond to their writings it is easier for them to use a word-based grammar. Naturally grammars based on modern linguistics may be able to tell us something different and perhaps equally valuable about a particular author's use of language, though in many instances it may well tell us something that the author himself was not aware of. Most authors, however, are supremely conscious of their vocabulary and spend considerable energy in trying to find the right word for a particular passage. In addition, traditional grammar uses a vocabulary and methodology which are less intimidating to the average user of the language than those associated with modern linguistics. This is because it is a methodology which is perhaps inherently simpler, but which is still found elsewhere. For example, dictionaries list the words in a language and then they indicate to which class or classes each word belongs. Not only does this reinforce our belief that words do have a nature which marks them out as belonging to a particular class, but it also makes us familiar with such classes as noun and verb. Furthermore, if we learn a foreign language, the grammar of that language is more likely to be explained within the framework of traditional grammar than of modern linguistics. The same is true if we learn an older language such as Latin or Old English. It is, therefore, quite sensible to be familiar with traditional grammar and to be able to apply it to modern English in order that we can make it match these other areas of language study. It would set modern English too far apart from older varieties of our language and all other modern languages if we used a modern terminology for the one and a traditional one for the others.

I do not wish to imply from this that modern linguistics has not made significant advances in our understanding of language; the new approaches will continue to enlarge our grasp of the potential of language. But much of it is too specialised and recondite for many users of the language. In addition, although modern linguistics may sometimes give the impression that traditional grammar is *passé*, some of the terminology modern linguistics uses has been developed from it. Thus in that branch of modern linguistics called transformational generative grammar one could easily come across such a symbolic representation of the make-up of a sentence as $S \rightarrow NP + VP$. Although the precise meaning of this formula is not my concern here, it is not too difficult to realise that the abbreviations represent what in traditional grammar are sentence, noun phrase and verb phrase respectively. Although modern grammars may not explain the abbreviations in this way, there is a clear relationship between the terminology they use and that in traditional grammar. This is hardly surprising since traditional grammar has a well-established terminology which it was natural that modern grammarians should build on in their own work. Many of the bases of traditional grammar have never really been discarded, even if this position is not revealed in modern grammars.

Finally it needs to be stressed that not all modern

grammars are based either exclusively or even principally on modern linguistic methodologies, even if much of the advanced research and critical discussion is carried on in them. The most complete modern grammar is *A Comprehensive Grammar of the English Language* by Professor Quirk and his colleagues, which is the second edition of *A Contemporary Grammar of English*. These grammars have spawned many smaller versions, which are used widely in England and abroad. This grammar uses an eclectic terminology, for it draws upon many traditional features which are filled out by modern terms. It would probably be difficult for a reader of this grammar to make much headway in understanding English unless he was familiar with the terminology and methodology of traditional grammar. So even today a speaker of English needs to be familiar with traditional grammar if he wishes to make sense of any dictionary or the most comprehensive grammar of the language. Furthermore, he will find it an invaluable tool in the analysis of literary texts. These are all important reasons for becoming familiar with the methodology of traditional grammar. Traditional grammar is not something that has been discarded even if some of the views we associate with it, such as prescription, are now unfashionable. It still has much to offer, and it is for this reason that I have chosen to present an introduction to its methodology and terminology in this book. I shall also expand some of that terminology by including terms from modern linguistics which can usefully be considered alongside it. It remains important for all speakers of the language to be familiar with at least one grammatical methodology if they want to know something about their language and how to use it. Traditional grammar remains the most accessible one and it is still the best to begin with. It can serve as the foundation for study into more advanced types of grammar.

1   Review of Word Classes

As we saw in the last chapter, in a word-based grammar the words in a language are divided into separate classes. These have traditionally been known as PARTS OF SPEECH, though that term is no longer satisfactory. The word *speech* is largely restricted nowadays to the spoken language, whereas we are more concerned in this book with the written form; and *parts* suggests that the sentence is the predominant unit which is being divided into its essential elements. So it is better to refer to the divisions into which the words fall as WORD CLASSES. There are nine word classes which are normally recognised in English: nouns, verbs, pronouns, adjectives, adverbs, conjunctions, prepositions, articles and interjections. However, some grammarians disagree over the precise number of these classes. This dispute has been caused partly by a comparison of English with Latin and partly because the boundaries between some of the classes are somewhat fuzzy. In Latin there is no class of articles, since they do not exist in that language; and so some early grammarians who were influenced by the model of Latin tried to suggest that the class of articles should not be recognised in English. But this is to carry the comparison between English and Latin to absurd lengths, since articles such as *the* clearly do exist in English. The problem of the boundaries between the various classes is more serious, and this is a matter to which we shall have to refer to during the course of this chapter. Briefly it might be said that in a word-based grammar it ought to be possible to devise a definition for each class which is based on the inherent nature and meaning of the words in that class. This is not possible in English because some words can belong to more than one class, and clearly a word cannot have a meaning and nature which restrict it to a single class if it can be a member of several classes. In languages which have inflexional endings, it is the endings which will usually determine in which class a word belongs. As English is not an inflexional language it is not possible to have a series of definitions which rely simply on the inherent nature and meaning of the words. Hence the definitions of the word classes in English are based on a number of different features and these features vary from one class to the next. It is hardly surprising, therefore, that these features should occasionally come into conflict and cause dispute as to what actually constitutes the class in question. However, although it is possible theoretically to argue over the precise definitions of the various word classes in English, in practice those who are familiar with the system of traditional grammar have little difficulty in allocating any word in the language to its class. So, although it is necessary to discuss the theoretical bases of the division into word classes, the actual decision over individual words is not likely to constitute a serious problem.

In definitions of word classes three features are employed. The first is the meaning of the word itself. If one compares *wood* and *wooden*, one can see that in the first case the word means something which is tangible and represents an entity which is complete in itself. The second refers to a quality, which needs something to which it can refer since it is not complete in itself. One can speak of *a wooden poem* or *a wooden leg*, but not of *wooden* by itself. The second is the formal qualities of the words in the class, for some classes can take endings or otherwise undergo certain changes according to their meaning or function. We can use the same pair of words as an example. *Wood* can have a plural form *woods*, and for this reason belongs to a different class from *wooden*, which cannot have a plural form *woodens*. The third refers to the function a class of word plays in the sentence or in any grouping of words. *Wood* and *wooden* differ in this respect as well, since it is possible to put *wood* as the subject of *is*, but not *wooden*. One can say *Wood is a useful material*, but one cannot use *wooden* in a similar position. In the past it was customary to rely principally on the meaning of the words to divide them into classes, but this is in most cases insufficient. A much better idea of the differences among the classes is obtained by using all three features in combination. In the rest of this chapter I shall go through the various classes pointing out their primary differences so that the concept becomes more familiar, and in the following chapters the classes will be discussed in greater detail and the relationship among them explored more thoroughly.

The most important class is the NOUN, a word derived from the Latin *nomen* meaning 'a name'. The noun is indeed often thought of as a naming word, though that is not a sufficient or complete definition. Traditionally, a noun is defined through its meaning as a word signifying a person, place or thing. From this definition nouns were divided into four categories: proper nouns, common nouns, abstract nouns and collective nouns. Of these it is the common noun which it is most difficult to categorise. A proper noun is one which refers to a particular individual or place, such as *Mr Smith* or *Sheffield*. These nouns are not preceded by *the* or *a(n)*, because there is only one specific individual or place with that name. Because of this such nouns are not normally found in the plural, for it there is only one London one cannot refer to more than one. But a surname can naturally refer to several members of a family, and so one can say *the Smiths*. An abstract noun, as its name implies, refers to an abstract entity or concept as distinct from something concrete. These words also are not normally found in the plural or preceded by *the* or *a(n)*, though they may be when a specific example of the concept is in question. Hence it is possible to have *Love is a wonderful emotion*, in which *love* as an abstract entity has no preceding *the* or *a*, as well as *The love which he had felt gradually ebbed away*, in which the specific love in question which is identifiable as a single thing does have *the* before it. A collective noun is one which refers to a group of people or things and regards them as a single undifferentiated mass. *Government* is a good example, for although a government consists of many members it is treated as a single unit. Because of their nature, collective nouns may be followed by a verb in the singular or plural: *The government has* (or *have*) *fallen*. Common nouns include all the nouns which do not fall into any of the other three sub-groups. In non-traditional grammatical systems nouns are divided into different sub-groups because it is sometimes difficult to decide whether a word is abstract or not. Should *love* be regarded as an abstract noun when it is preceded by *the*? The divisions in such grammars are made on more formal grounds, and we shall discuss them later. Even so, the division into proper, common, abstract and collective is one which most speakers of the language find helpful in discussions of the language.

As far as form is concerned, nouns are distinguished from other word classes by their ability to form a plural and a possessive form usually through the addition of an ending. The most common ending is *s*, which is used to form both the plural and the possessive forms. In writing apostrophes are also employed with the possessive *s*, though this is not a reflection of a difference at the spoken level. Hence *boy* has the further three forms *boy's* (possessive singular, meaning 'of or belonging to the boy'), *boys* (the plural, meaning 'two or more boys'), and *boys'* (the possessive plural, meaning 'of or belonging to the boys'). The three forms with the *-s* ending are pronounced in an identical way, and the apostrophes are merely matters of convenience in the written language to differentiate them. Not all words form the plural in the same way: some change their vowel (*man–men* and *foot–feet*); some do not change at all (*sheep–sheep*); and some have different endings altogether, particularly if they have been borrowed from other languages (*child–children* and *dilettante—dilettanti*). Such words still use the possessive form in *-s*. There are some endings which are restricted to nouns, such as *-ness* in, for example, *happiness*. Any word with one of these endings is a noun.

As for their function in a sentence, nouns are words which can act as the subject of a sentence. They precede the verb as subject and indicate who is doing the action of the verbs. In *The boy loves the girl* it is the boy which is the subject, for it is he who is doing the loving; and so *boy* is a noun. Nouns can fulfil other functions in the sentence than that of subject, as is true in the example given, for *girl* is not the subject of the sentence. But the important consideration is whether it is possible to make a sentence in which *girl* is the subject, such as *The girl loves the boy*. If a word can be the subject of a sentence rather than if it is the subject of a particular sentence, then it fulfils the necessary condition of this function. A noun can have other words which depend upon it. Common nouns usually have *the* or *a(n)* in front of them, and almost all nouns can have adjectives before them. In *the happy man*, both *the* and *happy* describe *man* and are dependent upon it. A noun can be dependent on another noun if it has the possessive form, as in *the boy's book*. Two nouns which are linked together must be separated by an *and*, or if there are more than two they must in writing be separated by a comma. A sentence which is written *Mercy, justice and humility are the highest virtues* is well-formed and makes sense, but if it had been written *Mercy justice humility are the highest virtues* it would not be considered acceptable. Nouns constitute an open class of words – that is, new nouns can be formed by any speaker of the language at will. The potential number of nouns in the language is infinite. New nouns are constantly arising through developments in technology. One has only to think of the new words associated with computing. In fact the noun class is perhaps the most open of all classes, for any word in the language can be made into a noun if it is made the subject of discussion. Although the word *if* is not a noun, it is possible to make it into one by writing *The if in the previous sentence is not a noun*.

A VERB is usually defined through its meaning as a word which indicates an action. This is clearly not a complete definition, for the word *action* itself is not a verb but a noun, and so many words would not be excluded by it. In addition some verbs, such as *is*, indicate a state rather than an action. It is necessary, therefore, to supplement the definition by some of the formal features of the verb. Verbs have more variations in their endings than any other word class. Consider the verb *to go*. In addition to the base form *go*, it has the following possible forms: *goes, went, gone* and *going*. This verb is unusual only in that it uses the form *went* as a past tense form of the base *go*. The four forms are used respectively for the third person singular of the present indicative, *he goes*, the past tense, *he went*, the past participle, *he has gone*, and the present participle, *he is going*. The precise meaning and use of these forms will be considered in a later chapter. Not all verbs have the same number of forms. Those which form the past tense in *-ed* also form the past participle in the same way. *Shopped* is the past tense and past participle of *to shop*. Some verbs have an unchanged form in the past tense and/or the past participle. Thus the verb *to hit* is *I hit* in the present tense and also in the past tense; and the past participle is also *hit* – for example, *he has hit*. A few verbs have an even wider range of forms, though they are exceptional. The verb *to be* has several forms in the present tense: *I am, he is* and *they are*. It also has two forms in the past tense: *he was* and *they were*. Another group of verbs, among which are those verbs known as auxiliaries, has a very restricted range of forms. Take, for instance, the verb *can*. It has no separate form for the third person singular; for we must say *he can*, and not *he cans*. Similarly it does not have a past or present participle at all: *canned* and *canning* are not acceptable forms. These verbs form a rather special category, which will have to be considered in greater detail later. Certain endings are restricted to verbs, and are often attached to nouns and adjectives to turn them into verbs. The most productive at present is almost certainly *-ise* (or *-ize*), which has been added to many words in the present century: *fraternise, galvanise* and *theorise* to name only a few. Words with such endings are verbs.

From a functional viewpoint it was usual to say that a verb is an essential part of the sentence and that no sentence is complete without one. In written English this is still a mark of a formal style, though in informal styles there may be many sentences in which a verb does not appear. In a sentence the function of a verb is to express the action which the subject does. In our earlier example *The boy loves the girl*, *boy* is the subject and the action which he is doing is expressed through *loves*, which is the verb. Although a verb has many different forms, which may express among other things when or how the action is performed, the basic structure of the sentence is not modified by such variations in form. It is normal in English sentences for the verb to follow the subject either immediately or very quickly, though it should be borne in mind that the subject can consist of more than just a noun, as we shall see in Chapter 2.

The meaning of PRONOUN is often said to be that of a word

which stands in place of a noun, and this definition is based on the etymology of the word, for pronoun comes from Latin *pro + nomen*, 'for or in place of a naming word'. This definition is not entirely satisfactory because it suggests that in any sentence where there is a noun it could be replaced by a pronoun. But a pronoun will replace not only the noun itself but all the words which are dependent upon it. In the phrase *a happy man*, where there is a noun *man* and other words associated with it, it is not possible just to substitute a pronoun for the noun; it is not possible to have *a happy he*. It is obligatory to replace the whole phrase by the pronoun so that *a happy man* becomes *he*. So when it is stated that a pronoun stands in place of a noun, we mean in place of a noun and all the words it governs. Even this definition does not cover all pronouns, for there are some which can hardly be said to stand in place of any noun. In the sentence *Who is coming tonight?*, *who* is a pronoun, but it would be extremely difficult to think of what noun it was replacing. The definition that pronouns stand in place of nouns does nevertheless indicate a feature of the meaning of pronouns – namely, that they do not in themselves provide, within the framework of the clause in which they appear, all the necessary information for identification. If instead of the sentence *The boy loves the girl* there was simply *He loves her*, it would not be possible to know who the *he* and *her* were from that sentence alone. We could identify them only through linking them with people who had been mentioned in the immediate context. This applies even more to the pronouns *I* and *you*, which in a conversation refer to the speaker and the person spoken to, and the reference will change every time the speaker changes. The *I* of my speech is not the same person as the *I* of your speech. Pronouns can only be understood from the context in which they appear; they have little inherent meaning because they point to other words or situations.

In form pronouns constitute a mixed group. Some of them can change their form more than nouns, so that, for example, there is a subject form *I*, a non-subject form *me*, and possessive forms *my* and *mine* for the pronoun referring to the first person singular. The same applies to *he* and *she*, for each has non-subject and possessive forms. The *you* and *it* pronouns, however, have the same form in subject and non-subject positions, but they have possessive forms *your* and *yours* and *its* respectively. A similar range of forms is found in the plural. The range of forms of other pronouns is more restricted. The pronoun *who* has a non-subject form *whom*, but it is probably true to say that it is not used much any more. It does have a possessive form *whose*, but no separate plural form. But *who* is restricted to animate referents, and *which* is used instead for non-animate ones.

Pronouns are divided into a number of sub-groups. The major sub-groups are personal, reflexive and possessive pronouns, since they exhibit the differences in person and gender. The personal pronouns are those which can act as subject or object of a sentence. The possessive pronouns act like the possessive form of the noun in that they indicate possession, as their name implies. Hence *my book* indicates possession, namely that the book belongs to me. Reflexive pronouns add *-self* (singular) or *-selves* (plural) to either the non-subject form of the personal pronoun, as in *himself*, or the possessive pronoun, as in *myself*. They are found principally after certain verbs or for emphasis. Relative pronouns such as *who* and *which* introduce relative clauses, which are those clauses which follow nouns and delimit their meaning in some way. In *the boy who lives next door* there is a relative pronoun *who* which introduces the relative clause *who lives next door*, which in turn delimits the meaning of *boy*, because it restricts which person *boy* could refer to. Interrogative pronouns are identical in form with the relative pronouns beginning with *wh*. But, whereas relative pronouns introduce relative clauses, interrogative pronouns introduce questions. In *the boy who lives next door*, there is a relative clause *who lives next door* referring to *boy*. By itself *Who lives next door?* is a question introduced by an interrogative pronoun; and the question has to have a question mark instead of a full-stop. Demonstrative pronouns correspond to demonstrative adjectives, except that, whereas in their adjective forms they precede a noun, as pronouns they stand by themselves. There are four forms: *this* and *that* (singular) and *these* and *those* (plural). *This* and *these* refer to something near, as compared with *that* and *those*, which refer to something more distant. In

Who made that remark? the *that* is an adjective because it is dependent upon the noun *remark*; but in *Who said that?* it is a pronoun because it is standing in place of a noun, which in this case might be something like *sentence* or *remark*. There are a number of other pronouns which are more difficult to categorise, except that they tend to be non-specific, or perhaps one might say universal. Typical examples are *everyone* or *anyone*. Finally it may be noted that there are negative forms for some pronouns. *Anyone* has the negative form *no one*. We cannot say *Anyone cannot come*; we have to say *No one can come*.

Pronouns belong to the closed group of vocabulary. This implies that no new pronouns can be created. There is a limited number of pronouns in the language and their number cannot be increased. On the contrary, historically their number has tended to decrease.

An ADJECTIVE is traditionally said to be governed by a noun. This definition has more to do with function than with meaning. This is because it is extremely difficult to produce a definition of an adjective which is comprehensive. It could be said that an adjective has a general meaning which needs a noun to provide a specific framework of reference. Thus *green* is an adjective denoting a particular colour, but it needs something to which it can refer, such as *baize*, for *green* is not something that has a reference entirely within itself. However, it is a characteristic feature of modern English that nouns have been converted into adjectives by the process of functional shift. Although *car* by itself is a noun, in *a car door* it is an adjective because it defines what kind of door it is. Adjectives formed through functional shift are rather different in their meaning and behaviour from other adjectives. Whereas one could say that *green* needs a noun to which to refer to make sense, this is not true of *car*.

Adjectives differ from nouns in that they have no plural or possessive forms. The adjective *happy* remains unchanged even if the noun it is governed by changes: *the happy man, the happy man's bicycle, the happy men*. However, adjectives do have endings, but these are used only to indicate degree through the comparative and superlative. These endings are *-er* and *est*, as in the series *happy, happier* (comparative) and *happiest* (superlative). However, these endings are used only for adjectives which have one or at most two syllables. Longer adjectives form their comparative and superlative by putting *more* (comparative) or *most* (superlative) in front. So the superlative of *beautiful* is *most beautiful* and not *beautifullest*. Thus *more* and *most* fulfil the same function as adverbs which qualify adjectives, as we shall see shortly. Those adjectives which have been formed from nouns through functional shift cannot have a comparative and superlative, because they do not generally represent qualities which can have degrees. *A car door* cannot be turned into *a carest door* or even *a most car door*. To that extent adjectives formed from functional shift are of a different nature from the more traditional adjectives. There are some endings which are characteristic of adjectives, the most productive of which is probably *-y*. Nouns are turned into adjectives through the addition of *-y*, so that *dough* becomes *doughy*. However, since other word classes, particularly nouns, can end in *-y* (in the pair *honest–honesty*, it is the noun which ends in *-y* and the adjective has no ending), the *-y* ending is not a defining feature of adjectives. Some endings, such as *-ful* and *-some*, are restricted to adjectives.

Within a sentence the function of an adjective is to limit the meaning of a noun and so in its position it comes before a noun. Its position is relatively fixed. We must write *a happy man*, not *a man happy*. There are only a few instances where an adjective can be placed after a noun. If there are two adjectives, then it is permissible to put them after the noun, though they will then be separated by an *and* and put within commas; *the princess, young and beautiful, arrived at last*. It is equally possible to have two or more adjectives in front of the noun, and then it is unnecessary to have an *and* and it is not possible to use commas to separate them from the noun: *The beautiful young princess arrived at last*. In principle it is possible to have as many adjectives before a noun as one wishes, but in practice it is unusual to have more than three. Adjectives may also be found by themselves after certain verbs, particularly the verb *to be*. *The happy man* may also be expressed as *The man is happy*. This is known as the predicative use of adjectives, and it can occur only after verbs which imply a state rather than an action, for it indicates a state of being which does not imply any progress or change. Adjectives which have been formed from nouns through functional shift cannot be placed in the predicative position. *A car door* cannot be changed into *A door is car*. Adjectives belong to the open classes of words, for we have already seen how easy it is to turn nouns into adjectives even if those nouns do not possess all the characteristics of traditional adjectives. New adjectives are perhaps not as common as new nouns, but rather more common than new verbs.

An ADVERB is traditionally said to be governed by a verb, just as an adjective is governed by a noun. This is not a complete definition, as adverbs may be used when they are governed by other word classes, particularly adjectives. Adverbs help to define and specify the meaning of a verb, and they therefore tend to answer questions such as 'How?' or 'When?' In the sentence *The boy is running* the verb is not particularised in any way. But it would be possible to ask how the boy was running, and then it would be necessary to introduce an adverb. The resulting sentence might then be *The boy is running quickly* or *The boy is running lazily*. Both *quickly* and *lazily* are adverbs because they indicate how the action of the verb is performed. The form of the adverb is varied. The most common form is the ending *-ly*, which is added to adjectives to transform them into adverbs. *Quickly* and *lazily* have the equivalent adjectives *quick* and *lazy*. But adverbs do not always need an *-ly*, for such a word as *fast* can be either an adjective or an adverb. In *a fast car* it is an adjective, but in *he drives fast* it is an adverb, for in the first it describes what kind of car it is, and in the second it describes how the driver is driving. It is not necessary to think of adverbs simply as modified adjectives, for other word classes can also be used as adverbs. For example, *tomorrow* is a noun in *tomorrow will never come*, for it is acting as the subject of the sentence. But in *He will come tomorrow* it is acting as an adverb, for it answers the question 'When?'

One type of adverb has an intensifying nature and it can be used with adjectives. In *a very happy man*, *happy* is an adjective but *very* is an adverb. It is clearly not an adjective because one cannot have *a very man*. The *very* intensifies the meaning of *happy* and answers the question 'How?' Not all adverbs can act as intensifiers to adjectives, and it might even be true to say that their number has decreased rather than increased recently. The same words which can intensify adjectives can also intensify adverbs. *He was running quickly* could be expressed as *He was running very quickly*. The form *very* is rather special in that it cannot be used by itself as an adverb; and this feature it shares with a restricted number of other words such as *extremely*. The use of unusual intensifying adverbs is now often regarded as a feature of poetic style. This intensifying adverb has a restricted position in a sentence in that it must come before the adjective or other word to which it refers. Adverbs which are governed by verbs are much freer in their position, for adverbs have of all word classes the greatest freedom of position. The following sentences are all possible in English:

1   He beat his wife regularly.
2   Regularly he beat his wife.
3   He regularly beat his wife.

The variation in word order can be used for stress and emphasis, though the order of the second sentence is less common than the other two. The only position where one does not usually find an adverb is between the verb and its object. It is not usual to write *He beat regularly his wife*. The adverb belongs to the open class of words, and new adverbs can be made by the addition of an -*ly* to an adjective. But this type of verbal enlargement is not encountered so frequently today.

The remaining four word classes may be dealt with a little more expeditiously, since they do not show the same variety in form or function as the major word classes. They all belong to the closed classes of words; new words cannot be invented for these classes. The two simplest classes are articles and interjections. There are only two ARTICLES in English; the indefinite article is *a* (or *an* before vowels) and the definite article is *the*. The indefinite article refers only to a type or class without specifying an individual within that type or class, whereas the definite article refers to a specific member of that class. *A boy* refers to the class without specifying which member of that class is involved, but *the boy* refers to a particular boy. *The* is used as the plural form of the definite article, though the plural of the indefinite article *a* is *some*. An INTERJECTION is a word which really stands outside the normal framework of a sentence and expresses feelings such as surprise, alarm or irritation. Words such as *Hello* and *Oh* fall into this class, as do many swear-words. In theory this class could be increased by the use of other word classes in this position, but in practice this does not happen very often. Interjections often exist as sentences on their own; it would not be surprising to find *Hello* as a sentence by itself. But they can also be found within a sentence, though they stand outside the structure of the rest of the sentence and are frequently marked off from it with an exclamation mark.

A PREPOSITION is so called because in Latin it means placed before something (*pre-* 'before', and *positio* 'position'); and a preposition is placed before a noun or one of the words governed by a noun. Prepositions express a relationship between one noun and another, as in *the house on the hill*, in which the *on* clarifies where the house is in relation to the hill. Their meaning is indicated through this relationship of two nouns. Their position and syntactic function are clearly circumscribed. They belong to the closed class of words for it is not usual to invent new prepositions. However, recently groups of words acting functionally as prepositions have become more common and their number may well increase. They include such groups as *on account of* and *with regard to*. Whereas prepositions express a relationship between nouns, CONJUNCTIONS express one between clauses or in some cases between word classes. They consist of two quite separate categories: co-ordinating and subordinating conjunctions. If there are two sentences such as *The boy threw a ball. The dog fetched it*, it is possible by using *and* to unite these to form a single sentence: *The boy threw a ball and the dog fetched it*. In this case the two halves of the sentence are of equal status; each clause can stand by itself. In this case *and* is a co-ordinating conjunction because it is uniting two clauses of the same status. But, if the sentence is rewritten *When the boy threw a ball, the dog fetched it*, the clauses are not of equal status because the first clause cannot stand by itself. Here the *when* makes the initial clause subordinate to the second one. It is not possible for *When the boy threw the ball* to stand by itself, because it is not a complete utterance. It needs something else to complete it. *When* is therefore said to be a subordinating conjunction. Subordinating conjunctions can be used only to join separate clauses together, but co-ordinating conjunctions are also used to join words of the same class together. In *He ran quickly and energetically*, the two adverbs are linked by *and*. When a conjunction links clauses together, the conjunction will stand at the head of its clause.

It may be most sensible to give a brief review of the points already made in this chapter regarding the differences between the word classes.

Open classes

NOUNS refer in meaning to a person, place or thing; they have a plural form, usually in *-s*, and a possessive in *-s*; and they can act as the subject of the sentence, though there are many other functions they can fulfil. As subject a noun will come at or near the beginning of a sentence.

VERBS are words indicating action, though some indicate a state; they have a variety of different endings, though each verb differs as to how many it has; they express the action which the subject does and they tend to follow the subject immediately in a sentence.

ADJECTIVES help to specify a noun more closely by adding some distinguishing feature; they have endings only in the comparative and superlative; and they are placed immediately before nouns or predicatively after certain verbs.

ADVERBS help to specify verbs by indicating how or when the action of the verb was done; they frequently end in *-ly*, but other forms are also found; and their position in the sentence is relatively free.

Closed classes

PRONOUNS stand in place of a noun and the words which depend upon it; they have a variety of different forms, including a subject, possessive and non-subject case; and they function in the same way in the sentence as nouns.

ARTICLES consist of only *the* and *a* (plural *some*) and they are placed before the noun and its accompanying adjectives, if any.

INTERJECTIONS express feelings such as surprise and are usually outside the normal framework of the sentence.

PREPOSITIONS express the relationship between nouns and are placed in front of a noun and its associated adjectives and articles, if any.

CONJUNCTIONS link clauses together, though co-ordinating conjunctions may also link words of the same class together; when linking clauses they occur at the head of the clause.

2   Nouns and Associated Word Classes

In the last chapter the traditional word classes were enumerated and features by which they could be recognised were listed. Some classes are more closely linked together than others, and it is useful to consider such classes together, particularly as they are treated together in more recent grammatical models. For example, part of the definition of an adjective is that it is governed by a noun, and so adjectives are almost invariably found next to a noun. Similarly, an article will only be found where a noun follows. So adjectives and articles may profitably be considered with nouns. One of the definitions of a noun given in the previous chapter was that it could act as the subject of a sentence. If we consider the following sentences, we can see which words are linked with the noun which is the subject. In each sentence the italicised part is the subject, while the predicate, i.e. that part of the sentence which is not the subject, remains the same. To that extent the italicised units are interchangeable.

1   *He* ran quickly.
2   *The boy* ran quickly.
3   *The biggest boy* ran quickly.
4   *The boy who lives next door* ran quickly.
5   *The biggest boy who lives next door* ran quickly.

In each sentence except the first *boy* appears in the subject. In that sentence *he* appears rather than *boy*. This *he* has to stand by itself, for it cannot be modified by any of the adjectives or other words used within the subjects of the other sentences. One cannot say *the biggest he*. Consequently, *he* stands instead of any of the subjects in the other sentences. In the other sentences *boy* remains the essential element in the italicised groups, for the other words depend upon it and if it were removed the sentences would in most cases become meaningless. It is possible, therefore, to think that each of these italicised units is a NOUN GROUP. This means that words of different classes can be joined together to form a group. The group will still fulfil the function of the essential word in it, and it may conveniently be labelled after the class of that word. A noun can fulfil the function of subject of a sentence, and so a group of words which acts as a subject may by extension be thought of as a noun group. This chapter will therefore be concerned with the word classes which are found in a noun group, and it will seek to provide more information about those classes than there was room for in the previous chapter.

A group may for the moment be defined as one or more words which carry out the function of a particular word class. If one function of the noun is to act as subject of a sentence, then a noun group will consist of those words which act as the subject of a sentence and thus fulfil the same function as a noun. Normally a group will contain a single word upon which the other words in the group depend; and this may be called the HEAD of the group. The words dependent upon the head may come either before or after it. In *the boy who lives next door*, it is not difficult to see that *boy* is the word upon which the other words depend. The words dependent on it include the single article *the* before and a group of words *who lives next door* after the head. The head of a noun group is almost always a noun or a pronoun; in the first example above, where *he* is found, it forms the noun group by itself. We shall start this chapter by considering the noun itself in more detail.

Although some features of the noun were elaborated in the previous chapter, others call for comment. As we saw, nouns can be divided into proper, common, abstract and collective, but there are sometimes difficulties in deciding into which category a particular noun fits. If a proper noun is defined as a word which refers to a particular person or place, it is clear that *Mr Smith* is a proper noun for it refers to a single individual. If we refer to *the Smiths*, would that be a proper noun or a common noun, for normally a proper noun can have no plural form as there cannot be more than one of a particular person or place? Because of this difficulty, it has become usual to extend the traditional word class by dividing nouns into more formal categories. A division of nouns into count and non-count nouns separates those nouns which can be counted from those which cannot. As a general rule count nouns take the article *the*. *The boy* has the plural form *the boys*, because boys can be counted, but *revenge* does not have a plural form *revenges* for it cannot be counted. The former is a count noun, and the latter a non-count noun. Even this formal division has some drawbacks, for collective nouns can take *the* but not all are count nouns. *The cattle* cannot have a plural form and so is a non-count noun, but *the government* can and so must be treated as a count noun.

The plural in English is basically a matter of number: the singular indicates one and the plural more than one. Non-count nouns are generally followed by the verb in the singular, though number is not involved in these words in that they have no plural for they signify an undifferentiated mass which may be either large or small. Consequently non-count nouns are sometimes referred to as mass nouns. In the negative, number is not involved since the absence of something does not differentiate between singular and plural. The following sentences do not differ in meaning:

1 No book may be taken out of the library.
2 No books may be taken out of the library.

Some nouns have a plural form in special senses which may in practice differ little from the equivalent singular. Thus in *The heavens opened* or *The hopes and fears of all the years are met in thee* it is not possible to substitute the singular form for the plural nouns. Some words, such as *trousers* and *scissors*, exist only in a plural form, though they have a singular meaning. Adjectives which are turned into nouns often have no plural ending in -*s*, though they may be plural in meaning and can take a verb in the plural, as in *The poor are always with us*.

A feature of the noun is that it can have a possessive form in *-s* (in the singular with the apostrophe before and in the plural with the apostrophe after it). This possessive form is now restricted to animate nouns and to certain set phrases, but in the past it was available to all nouns. As the sense of possession has grown stronger with this form, it is now used only with those nouns which can physically possess something. So we can speak of *the boy's book* but not of *the house's windows*, for a house can hardly be said to own or possess the windows in it. A different way of expressing possession is to use an *of* phrase following the noun so that *the boy's book* may be turned into *the book of the boy*. This form of expression is available for non-animate nouns as in *the windows of the house*. Presumably the sense of possession is not so marked with the *of* phrase, and the preposition used may vary from *of* to *in* or whatever. *The windows in the house* is just as acceptable as *the windows of the house*. Because the *of* phrase is clumsy and time-consuming, English has developed the strategy of using nouns which cannot take the possessive *-s* as adjectives. Although it is not possible to have *the house's door*, it is perfectly in order to use *the house door*, where *house* acts as an adjective to the noun *door*. Animate nouns which can use the possessive form with *-s* are not normally found in the adjective position without *-s*; *the boy's book* cannot be transformed into *the boy book*. Only with those nouns in which the feeling of animacy is not clear-cut can both forms be found. A good example is *government*, which can be thought of as both animate and inanimate. So one may use both *the government position* and *the government's position*. In traditional phrases nouns which are not animate still retain an *-s* form, though in these cases possession is not usually implied. In phrases such as *a stone's throw* or *a day's work*, the meaning is 'as far as a stone can be thrown' and 'the work which can be done in a day' respectively. Such traditional phrases merely show that in the past the sense of possession was not so marked with the *-s* form of nouns, but it has become so as it has been increasingly restricted to animate nouns.

This sense of possession has affected the meaning of the *-s* form. When we today say *the boy's fear* we now mean that the boy feared something: it is the boy who is doing the fearing.

Earlier in English it was possible to understand *the boy's fear* in a different way, for it could mean the fear that other people had for the boy. In that case it was not the boy who was fearing; he was being feared. This usage is now much less common than it used to be, and what in the past could have been expressed as *God's fear* must now be represented as *the fear of God*. With the *of* phrase this ambiguity also remains because *the fear of the boy* can mean either the fear he feels or the fear which others feel for him, though it is probably true to say that the latter is the dominant meaning.

Because some nouns cannot have the possessive form in *-s* and have consequently been converted into adjectives, the question naturally arises as to how it may be decided when a noun is a noun and when it is an adjective. The answer is through the word order. Although in the past the position of the adjective was flexible, today an adjective will come before its noun. The traditional phrase *little boy blue* shows that in the past it was possible to put the adjective *blue* after the noun *boy*. But one only has to try to substitute *white* for *blue* to understand how fossilised this phrase is and how impossible it is to use it as a model for other phrases. Although poets still exploit this freedom of placing an adjective after the noun often to create ambiguity, it is precisely to avoid such ambiguity in ordinary language that the word order has become restricted.

If we consider the fifth example quoted at the beginning of this chapter, *The biggest boy who lives next door ran quickly*, the subject or noun group consists of *The biggest boy who lives next door*. In this group it is *boy* which is the head, for the other words are dependent upon it. In this group it is possible to see that the head is preceded only by single words, both *the* and *biggest*, which both relate to *boy* but which do not depend upon each other. The head *boy* is followed by a group of words which are mutually dependent. In *who lives next door* it would not be possible to eliminate *who* or *lives* and still have a grammatical expression. It is also not possible to organise these units the other way round: *the boy biggest* is as ungrammatical as *the who lives next door boy*. It is important to understand that single-word units come before the head and multiple-word units after it, because the head of a noun group which has more than one word in it is a noun. This organisation enables us to know which word is that noun, for it will be the last of the single-word units in a noun group. For example, *the motor car* and *the car motor* are two quite separate things because of this rigidity of English word order. In *the motor car*, *car* is the last single word and must be the noun; this noun group means a car driven by a motor (rather than by a horse or some other means of propulsion). In *the car motor*, it is *motor* which is the last single word and so it must be a noun; and the group means a motor used in a car (rather than in an aeroplane). By the same token, in *the motor car*, *motor* is an adjective, as is *car* in the group *the car motor*. Because of this word order in English we can understand newspaper headlines, which often use what appear to be only nouns joined together. Consider the following groups of words which could easily appear in headlines and which would cause no difficulty in comprehension to the average speaker of the language.

1   Power strike.
2   Power strike gamble.
3   Power strike gamble fiasco.

In each group it is the last word which is the noun, because each group consists only of single-word units. The preceding words have to be understood as adjectives which are governed by the noun. In the first phrase *strike* is a noun, and *power* is an adjective which explains what kind of strike it was; it was a strike involving the supply of power at the power stations rather than a strike on the railways. In the second group *gamble* is the noun and the two preceding words are adjectives, and the meaning is a gamble which was taken with reference to the power strike. In the third phrase *fiasco* is the noun, and the preceding three words are adjectives with the overall meaning of the fiasco which resulted from the gamble taken in the power strike.

Although the arrangement outlined in the previous paragraph is standard in Modern English, there are inevitably one or two exceptions. There are some cases in which an adjective can follow a noun. The first is when there are two adjectives linked by *and*. These can follow the noun, but when they do so they are in writing marked off from it by commas: *The house, grim and foreboding, was picked out by the moonlight*. This structure is literary and is largely confined to written examples. The second is when the adjective is a participle, which is an adjective formed from a verb and normally ends in either *-ed* or *-ing*. In *The matters discussed cannot be made public*, *discussed* is a participial adjective referring to *matters*. It is formed from the verb *to discuss* by the addition of the ending *-ed*. This type of construction has influenced one or two other cases where adjectives which are not participles may follow the noun, as for example in *The information available is restricted*. The third case in which an adjective can follow the noun consists of examples where the adjective is formed from an adverb through functional shift. In *The sentence above is ungrammatical*, *above* must be understood as an adjective agreeing with the noun *sentence*. This word does not occur commonly as an adjective, and has been formed from the adverb *above*. It is possible to rewrite this last example as *The above sentence is ungrammatical*, but this order is at present less usual. That these adjectival functions are somewhat separate from the common ones is suggested by the fact that they can be used with pronouns. One cannot say *Beautiful she waited for him*; but it is acceptable to have *She, beautiful and silent, waited for him*.

Although it is right to analyse groups such as *motor car* in the way outlined above, it has to be mentioned that many speakers of the language are uncertain whether to write *motor car* as one word or two. One can find it written as *motor car, motor-car* or *motorcar*. If one of the two latter forms is used then the resulting form would be understood as a single word and would be interpreted as a noun. The more common an expression is, the more likely it is that it will be written as a single word. At a spoken level, the stress pattern will often be a guide as to whether the speaker is thinking of one or two words. For example, when *blackbird* is a single word there is more stress on *black* than *bird*; but when there are two words, *black bird*, there will be more stress on *bird*. This is because, although the tendency in English is to put the stress at the beginning of words, in groups the stress is likely to fall on the principal element, which in the noun group will be its head. It is hardly surprising that there should be some uncertainty in this matter, because as expressions become more common they move from an adjective-plus-noun combination to a single noun. You have only to think of all the words which can go in front of *bin*, for example, such as *dust, bread* and *swing*, to realise how uncertain the arrangement into one or two words is. Grammatically, however, there is no problem, since whether there are two words or one the resulting expression is analysed in accordance with the principles which have been laid out earlier.

There are occasions when an adjective consists of more than one word. We noted in the last chapter that adjectives can have comparative and superlative forms, so that *big* has the forms *bigger* and *biggest*. However, when an adjective consists of more than two syllables, the comparative and superlative are formed by the use of *more* and *most*, so that *beautiful* has the forms *more beautiful* and *most beautiful*. It is not possible to have *beautifuller* and *beautifullest*. In the case of *more beautiful* the adjective may be said to consist of two words the first of which is an adverb which strengthens or intensifies the meaning of the adjective; and hence it is often referred to as an INTENSIFIER. Intensifiers are not restricted to *more* and *most* forming the comparative and superlative, for there are many other words which can be used in a similar way. One of the most common is *very*. That intensifiers belong to the adjective rather than to the noun or head of the noun group is easy to appreciate. In the noun group *a very beautiful girl*, the *very* clearly belongs with *beautiful* and not with *girl*. One cannot say *a very girl*, because *very* is an adverbial intensifier which can only intensify an adjective; it is not an adjective which can be used to describe a noun. In cases where there is an intensifier it may be said to form a two-word PHRASE with the following adjective, and together they can be referred to as an ADJECTIVE PHRASE. This phrase behaves like a single adjective and follows the normal word order associated with adjectives. Some words, such as *very*, can only be intensifiers and so there is no difficulty about their interpretation. But a few words may be either intensifiers or adjectives, and when they are used there may be ambiguity as to the meaning of the resulting group. For example, in *a lovely red rose*, *lovely* is a word that can be either an intensifier or an adjective. In the former case it would mean a rose that was of a lovely red colour; and in the latter a rose that was both lovely and also red. In this case most people would probably understand the group to have the second rather than the first interpretation. Ambiguity may be avoided in speech through intonation and stress, and in writing through the use of a comma.

Adjectives are of different kinds. We have already seen that some may be formed through functional shift from nouns. Because some people find it difficult to think of nouns as adjectives, the technical word MODIFIER is sometimes used for any word which can be put in front of the head of a noun group, whether it is a traditional adjective or an adjective formed from a noun. Even traditional adjectives are of different types, depending on what aspect of the noun they refer to. Some indicate how many of the noun(s) there are and these are called adjectives of number; they include words such as *one* and *two*. Others indicate what the features of the noun are and are referred to as adjectives of quality; they include such words as *lovely* and *elegant*. Some refer to the colour of the noun and are naturally referred to as adjectives of colour; they include such words as *red*. The differences in the types of modifier or adjective which are found in English are significant principally for the word order, though they also have some bearing on the use of *and*. Adjectives do not have a free arrangement in the order they occupy before the head of the noun group. It is not acceptable to write *the elegant two houses*, because adjectives of number precede adjectives of quality. It must be written *the two elegant houses*. The preferred order in English is that adjectives of number come before all other adjectives. Then adjectives of colour usually precede adjectives of quality. All these adjectives come before modifiers which have been turned from nouns into adjectives through functional shift. One cannot have *two period elegant houses*, for the modifier *period* which is formed from a noun must come immediately before the head of the group; the accepted order is *two elegant period houses*. When two adjectives of the same kind appear together, they may occur in any order.

When that does happen it is possible, and may sometimes be obligatory, to separate the two adjectives by *and*, whereas normally the adjectives which occur before a noun do not need an *and* to separate them, as can be seen from the examples already used in this paragraph. The reason for this will be appreciated by comparing the two sentences: *The blue black pens were stolen* and *The blue and black pens were stolen*. In the latter example there are *blue pens* and *black pens*, but in the former *blue* is understood as an intensifier to *black* and the two might often be written as a compound *blue-black*. Even where the interpretation of one adjective as an intensifier is not very likely, two adjectives of the same kind will usually be separated by an *and* in order to prevent possible ambiguity. Thus one would write *This is a scholarly and witty book* rather than *This is a scholarly witty book*. In poetic language the *and* may be omitted precisely to allow for the ambiguity which we prefer to avoid in ordinary discourse.

In the previous chapter the class of articles was introduced; it consists only of *a* and *the*, though the former has the plural *some*. *Some* differs from the two other articles in that it can stand by itself as a pronoun, whereas *a(n)* and *the* must always appear before a noun. Although one can say *Give me some*, one cannot say *Give me a* or *Give me the*. The two singular articles are very restricted in their use. A little reflection will reveal that there is a close relationship between *a(n)* and *one* and between *the* and *this/that*. There is little or no difference between *Give me one apple* and *Give me an apple*; and equally there is little or no difference between *The boy over there* and *That boy over there*. The major difference is a formal one in that *a(n)* and *the* must appear before a noun, but *one* and *this/that* need not, so it would be perfectly possible to have such sentences as *Give me one* and *Give me that*. To put it a different way, one could say that *one* and *this/that* can act as the heads of a noun group, but *a(n)* and *the* cannot. But when *this* or *that* acts as the head of a noun group it is a pronoun and cannot be modified by an article or by an adjective: one cannot have *the this* or *the fat this*. It is clear, then, that there is a much closer relationship now between *the* and *this/that* than between *a(n)* and *one*. In fact one can replace *the* by *this* or *that* and it is helpful to have a term which covers not only the articles, but also the other words which can occupy the same position in the noun group as *the*. The term now used is DETERMINER.

It is possible to categorise determiners in the following way. They come before the head of a noun group, and when there are modifiers as well in a noun group the determiner will also come before them. In other words the order of a noun group is determiner–modifier(s)–head. There will only be one determiner, which means that determiners are mutually exclusive. If you have one determiner, you cannot have others with it. It is possible to have *the happy man* and *this happy man*, but not *the this happy man*. It is apparent that there are differences between *the* and *this* other than the ability of *this* to stand by itself as a pronoun. Even when it acts as a determiner, *this* has to change its form (to *these*) when it stands before a noun in the plural, although this does not apply to *the*. Although *the* does not change in the groups *the happy man* and *the happy men*, *this* must in the same position change to *these*, so that *this happy man* becomes *these happy men*.

The determiners do not form an entirely coherent group, for some, such as the articles, can appear only before the head of a noun group, but others, such as *this* and *that*, can appear as pronouns by themselves. Some, such as the possessive pronouns, have one form as determiner and a second form as pronoun, so that one may say *This is my book*, but *my* becomes *mine* in the predicative form *This book is mine*. Equally determiners are restricted in their use. Some occur only before singular nouns such as *a*, *each* and *every*; others occur only before plural nouns such as *some* and *both*; and yet a third group can occur before either singular or plural, though sometimes the form may be changed. As we have seen, not all nouns take a determiner. The principal characteristic of a determiner is that within its class it is mutually exclusive: one determiner cannot be used next to another. This is a relatively recent restriction in English, for in the Prayer Book one can find archaic expressions such as *these our sins* where two determiners occur together. This usage is no longer possible in standard English.

I have indicated that within the noun group the normal

order is determiner–modifier(s)–head, as in the group *the happy man*. There can in theory be as many modifiers as one wishes, though in practice the number tends not to exceed three. There will naturally be only a single determiner, because of the rule that determiners are mutually exclusive. There are two other types of word which may occur in this initial part of the noun group. They are called INTENSIFIERS and PRE-DETERMINERS in modern grammars; the former has already been explained, though a few additional words may be in order. It is not possible to have a group of words such as a phrase acting as a modifier in English, so that, although it is possible to say *the girl with the beautiful eyes*, it is not possible to say *the with the beautiful eyes girl*. In some cases it may be possible to have a group of words acting together as a modifer, but when that happens it is customary to hyphenate the words together to make it appear as though they form a single word. Hence we write *a never-to-be-forgotten experience* or *a once-in-a-lifetime opportunity*, though it must be said that these hyphenated groups acting as modifiers are not common. However, it is possible to qualify a modifier by a word which restricts its meaning in some way. Thus *generous* can be qualified as *very generous*, *extremely generous* or even *wonderfully generous*. These words, such as *very, extremely* and *wonderfully*, are called adverbs in traditional grammar because they have, for the most part, the adverbial ending in *-ly*. Adverbs of course are normally thought of as qualifying verbs, but in the case of a noun group they qualify adjectives. It is for this reason that they are in modern grammars referred to as intensifiers, because they can be thought of as intensifying the modifier they qualify. To that extent they can, like many adverbs, be thought of as answering the question 'How?' If someone runs quickly, one may say *How does he run?*, for which the answer is *quickly*. Equally, if someone is good, one can ask the question *How good is he?*, to which the answer is *very good*. Intensifiers are unusual in that they are not linked by a hyphen to the modifier, for as we have just seen there is a convention in English that modifiers consist of a single word. Intensifiers form the exception to that rule. There is normally only a single intensifier to any one modifier, though in colloquial language the intensifier may be repeated for extra emphasis, as in *You're very, very naughty*. That this type of reduplication may have been commoner at an earlier stage of the language is suggested by Hamlet's *too too solid flesh*.

The category of pre-determiner in more modern grammars is one for which no exact equivalent exists in traditional grammar, though the few words which can act as pre-determiner would be classified as adjectives. The name pre-determiner arises naturally from the position of the word. If there is a noun group such as *the happy boys* which consists of determiner, modifier and head, it is possible to have a word in front of the determiner to give such a group as *half the happy boys*. It is clear that *half* does not refer either to *happy* or to *boys*; the meaning is elliptical for *half the number of happy boys*. It certainly does not mean *the half-happy boys* or *the happy half boys*. It is for this reason that *half* appears in the position it does. The words which occur as pre-determiners usually indicate number in some way. Another group of words may occur in the same position, but they are of a rather different nature since they are more like adverbs than adjectives. These words include *just, really* and *only*, as in *He's just a boy*; but they can also be used in different situations, as in *He's just arrived*. They are, therefore, better considered as outside the noun group.

So far we have decided that the noun group can consist of the following elements: pre-determiner, determiner, modifier and head. There will be only one pre-determiner and one determiner before a head. There may be several modifiers, though the number is not likely to be more than three. Usually there is only a single head, though it is possible to have more than one head joined with *and*. When this happens it is now customary not to repeat the determiner, though this happened quite regularly at an earlier stage of the language and may still be done when the two heads are some way apart in meaning. Thus we say *the men and boys* rather than *the men and the boys*. When a co-ordinate head has a modifier it is not always possible to decide whether the modifier belongs to one or to both the heads. In *the young men and boys* one might assume that *young* referred only to *men*; but in *the happy men and boys* one might think that *happy* referred to both *men* and *boys.* Generally each of the elements of the noun group listed above is represented by a single word; the exception to this is the modifier, which may be qualified by an intensifier as in *the very young men.* As we saw in the examples at the beginning of this chapter it is possible to have elements in a noun group after the head. One example quoted there was *The boy who lives next door.* Here there is a number of words which are mutually dependent after the head, *boy.* Because this arrangement differs from that for modifiers, it was possible to introduce the general principle that the elements before the head in a noun group are each represented by a single word, whereas those after it are represented by more than one word. Only in the rather rare examples, such as an adjective after the noun, which were discussed earlier does one find a single-word unit after the head. It has seemed appropriate in modern grammars to distinguish the modifier which comes before the head from the multiple-word unit which comes after it, and this latter element is now called a QUALIFIER.

Because a qualifier consists of several words, it will normally be either a phrase or a clause – that is, a group of words with or without a verb. Consider the following two sentences:

1   *The girl with the beautiful hair* lives round the corner.
2   *The girl who has the beautiful hair* lives round the corner.

In each sentence the italicised words form the subject of the verb *lives.* In the first example the head *girl* is followed by a group of words without a verb. There is simply the phrase (which is essentially a group of words without a verb) *with the beautiful hair.* It is characteristic of these phrases to be made up of a preposition and what could be thought of as another noun group; in this case the preposition is *with* and the other noun group is *the beautiful hair.* Together they can be thought of as constituting a PREPOSITIONAL PHRASE. A qualifier which is a phrase is most likely to be a prepositional phrase, consisting of a preposition and a noun group. This introduces a new concept into our discussion, since it is the first time we have seen a noun group within another noun group. In order to avoid the problem of having one noun group dependent on another I shall refer to the subordinate one as a NOUN PHRASE. This means that a noun group acts functionally within a sentence as a subject or object, but a noun phrase is a subordinate element of a noun group. The noun group which is the subject of *lives* is *the girl with the beautiful hair*, and that consists of a determiner, *the*; a head, *girl*; and a qualifier, *with the beautiful hair*. But the qualifier itself consists of a preposition and a noun phrase. It is not difficult to realise that *the beautiful hair* could be an independent noun group and act as the subject of its own sentence, as for example in *The beautiful hair was cut off as a punishment*. But in *the girl with the beautiful hair* it acquires a subordinate role by acting as part of the qualifier to the head of a noun group. As the qualifier is the only part of a noun group to contain more than a single word, noun phrases will occur only in the qualifier position. But a noun phrase consists of the same elements as noun groups; in this case *the beautiful hair* is made up of a determiner, *the*; a modifier, *beautiful*; and a head, *hair*.

In the second example the head *girl* is followed by a group of words with a verb, namely *who has the beautiful hair*. These words constitute a clause, which consists of a subject, *who*; a verb, *has*; and an object, *the beautiful hair*. A clause differs from a phrase in containing a verb as an essential element within itself. A clause consists of the same elements as a sentence, but may, as in this instance, form a subordinate element within a sentence. It would be possible for the clause *who has the beautiful hair* to stand as an independent sentence, though in that case it would be a question and should be followed by a question mark. When it is treated as a qualifier, the clause will naturally be subordinated to the head of a noun group. In traditional grammar this clause is known as a relative clause, because it is introduced by the relative pronoun *who*.

Qualifiers add information to the head and thus usually provide more specific details about it. Although they characteristically consist of prepositional phrases or relative clauses, these are by no means the only types of qualifier which exist. Any group of words which depends upon and follows the head will constitute a qualifier to that head. One type which occurs quite frequently in literary texts, though it is not confined to them by any means, is that which has no specific word such as *who* or *with* to express the relationship between it and the head of the noun group. Usually in writing this type of qualifier will be marked off by commas, as in *Elizabeth, our beloved queen, will visit the hospital tomorrow.* Here *our beloved queen* is said in traditional grammar to stand in APPOSITION to the noun which is the subject of the sentence. The noun phrase *our beloved queen* is a qualifier to the head *Elizabeth* for it adds further information about it. It would have been possible to express the same idea through a relative clause as in *Elizabeth who is our beloved queen*, though that is considered a little clumsy because of its length. Without the *who is*, the only way that *our beloved queen* can be understood to refer to Elizabeth is through the word order and contextual meaning. In standard modern prose there is normally no difficulty in understanding which words act as a qualifier even though there may be no words which specifically link them to the head; and an expansion of the words to a relative clause by the addition of *who/which is/are* will normally resolve any difficulties. In poetry, however, there may be difficulties in interpreting whether certain words are qualifiers or not, because of the employment of metaphor and of the disruption of standard word order.

Although a noun group has usually no more than three modifiers, it can have any number of qualifiers. There may be a psychological explanation for this phenomenon in that modifiers provide information about something (i.e. the head) which has not yet been reached in the sentence. It may be that we do not like to store too much information in our minds without knowing to what it refers. Once the head has been reached, it is easy to add more and more information about it incrementally in the form of qualifiers. The only time a large number of modifiers is used is in abuse, when part of the point of delaying the head is wondering precisely what it will be, though the referent (i.e. the person being abused) is in practice already known. A good example occurs in Shakespeare's *Henry IV, Part I* where Prince Hal says of and to Falstaff: *Wilt thou rob this leathern-jerkin, crystal-button, not-pated, agate-ring, puke-stocking, caddis-garter, smooth-tongue Spanish pouch?* (II.iv.68–70), where *pouch* is the head for eight modifiers.

This example is exceptional, for the norm in English is to have a few modifiers and a long list of qualifiers so that information is added after rather than before the head. If the noun group is to be expanded, it will normally happen through the provision of more qualifiers, so that trailing noun groups are characteristic of English. It is, however, so easy to add qualifiers that one has to take care that the resulting expression does not become clumsy and unintelligible. English allows such sentences as *Get the book in the bookcase in the room with the yellow door at the end of the corridor on the ground floor of the south wing of our building*, where everything after *book* is adding information about it in the form of a qualifier. Or rather it raises the question of how many qualifiers there are.

This is a question that needs a little further discussion. When a head is followed by several prepositional phrases which form a qualifier it is not always easy to decide precisely what each prepositional phrase refers to. In the noun group *the parcel on the seat with the damaged corner*, it is possible to understand *with the damaged corner* as referring either to *the parcel* or to *the seat*. In the first case the parcel would both be on the seat and have a damaged corner; and in the second case the parcel would be on the seat which has a damaged corner. In the first case one would say that the head *parcel* has two qualifiers, the first being *on the seat* and the second being *with a damaged corner*; and it would be possible to arrange these qualifiers either in the order given or in the order *the parcel with the damaged corner on the seat*. In the second case one must analyse the head *parcel* as having a single qualifier, which is *on the seat with the damaged corner*, and no other word order would be possible. In this latter interpretation *on the seat with the damaged corner* is a single qualifier to *parcel*, and it is made up of a prepositional phrase consisting of the preposition *on* and the noun phrase *the seat with the damaged corner*. This noun phrase in its turn consists of a determiner *the*, a head *seat*, and a qualifier *with the damaged corner*. In other words *with the damaged corner* is a qualifier to a head (i.e. *seat*) which is itself part of a qualifier to a different head (i.e. *parcel*). It may be difficult to avoid this potential ambiguity in the reference of qualifiers, but a rearrangement of the word order may help. Unless the context militates against it, most speakers of English are likely to understand a given prepositional phrase to refer to the immediately preceding noun, so that in the example *the parcel on the seat with the damaged corner* it is probable that most people will understand *with the damaged corner* to refer to *seat*.

It is possible to have qualifiers of different organisational structure referring to the same head. So the example from the previous paragraph could be modified to *the parcel on the seat which is wrapped up in yellow paper and tied with pink string*. Since it is unlikely that a seat would be wrapped up in this way, it would be assumed that the head *parcel* has two qualifiers, the first *on the seat*, and the second *which is wrapped up in yellow paper and tied with pink string*. The first of these is a prepositional phrase and the second a relative clause. The implication of this order may well be that there are several parcels on the seat and one wants to specify a particular one.

To summarise what has been set out in this chapter, we can say that a noun group consists of the following parts: pre-determiner, determiner, modifier(s), head and qualifier(s). The head is the only essential element of a noun group and it may often appear by itself. If the head is a pronoun, that will almost invariably be the case. The number of words that can occupy the pre-determiner and determiner slots is limited, and there will be only one of each category before a given head. In principle there can be as many modifiers as one wishes before a head, though in practice there are unlikely to be more than three. Modifiers consist of single words, though their meaning can be specialised through intensifiers. Qualifiers are made up of groups of words and are most likely to be either prepositional phrases or relative clauses. There is no limit to the number of qualifiers which follow a head, though it may sometimes be difficult to decide whether a particular qualifier refers directly to the head of the noun group or to a head of a subordinate noun phrase which is part of a qualifier to the main head. The abundance of qualifiers means that noun groups can be expanded almost indefinitely, and this has meant that in English literature it is the noun group which has traditionally carried the stylistic heightening which some writers have wished to achieve in their work. The previous sentence is an example of that tendency.

3 The Verb and its Constituents

It was noted in the first chapter that a verb is that word which indicates the action performed by the subject. But, just as the function of a noun can be accomplished by several words referred to as a noun group, so also the action performed by a verb can be indicated by several words which can on analogy be known as a VERB GROUP. This may be illustrated by the following examples:

1 Dorinda *laid* the table.
2 Dorinda *was laying* the table.
3 Dorinda *laid out* her plans.
4 Dorinda *was laying out* her plans.

In each of these examples the italicised words represent the action performed by the subject, *Dorinda*. In only the first one is that action represented by a single word. In the other examples there is a word before the main verb element or a word after it or in the fourth sentence a word both before and after it. It is important to realise in the third and fourth examples that *out* belongs with the verb group; it is not part of *her plans* which follows. Here *out* is not a preposition and one cannot understand *out her plans* as forming a unit of language. The *out* belongs with *lay*, and *lay out* is a separate verb from *lay* and has a different range of meanings. As a verb group *laid out* could be replaced by a single verb; in one of its senses it could be substituted by *explained*. A verb group, therefore, resembles a noun group in that it has a head which can be preceded and followed by other elements.

It differs from the noun group in that the head can vary its form considerably, usually depending upon the words which precede it in the verb group. We can refer to the three parts of the verb group as AUXILIARY, which is the word or words preceding the head; HEAD, which contains the main meaning of the verb group and upon which the other elements depend; and EXTENSION, which is the word or words which come after the head and modify its meaning. As with the noun group, the head is the only essential element of a verb group. The verb group may be thought of as somewhat less complicated structurally than the noun group since it consists of only these three elements.

The head of the verb group can appear in different forms. Almost all verbs in English distinguish between a present form and a past form, as in *write* and *wrote*, or *walk* and *walked*. These are traditionally known as present and preterite tenses because they refer to what is happening at the present time as in the case of *write* and *walk* or to what has happened in the past as in the case of *wrote* and *walked*. Originally these were the only two tenses in English, which is why they form the only two examples of tenses in which the head changes its form. When this was so, reference to other times was through adverbs. This is still possible in English, for one can say *The train arrives at midnight*, in which the present tense form *arrives* indicates a time in the future because of the adverb *at midnight*, which in this instance indicates a time in the future. Hence the two tense forms in English tended to suggest a past and a non-past time. However, during the development of modern English it has become possible to refer to other times through the use of one or more auxiliaries. It would be possible to express the previous example as *The train will arrive at midnight*, in which there is an auxiliary *will* and the head *arrive*. As such examples involve an auxiliary, they are rather different from those with the two original tenses, which involve a change in the form of the head. From the examples quoted earlier in this paragraph, it is apparent that there are two main ways in which the form of the verb in the present tense may be altered to provide the preterite tense. In the pair *write/wrote* the vowel *i* is changed to *o* to form the preterite and nothing is added to the word; but in

the pair *walk/walked* the ending *-ed* is added to the present to
form the preterite, but no change of vowel is carried out
within the verb. In a few verbs the *-ed* may appear as *-t*.
Traditionally these two verb types have been known
respectively as STRONG and WEAK verbs: the strong verbs
change the root vowel and the weak verbs add the ending *-ed*.
However, this terminology is not much used any more, and it
is more characteristic to refer to the different types of verb as
REGULAR and IRREGULAR. The strong verbs are the irregular
ones. The reason for this is that the majority of verbs in
English now form their preterite by adding *-ed*, and this is
certainly true of all new verbs. If you were to invent a new
verb today, it would form its preterite by adding an *-ed*. Thus
if *dinner* were to be turned into a verb, just as *lunch* has been,
its preterite would be *dinnered* and there would be no question
of its changing the vowel *i* to form a preterite. The ending *-ed*
is thus the living and the regular way of forming the preterite.
The irregular verbs which change their vowels represent a
small and diminishing group. They were once much more
common, as the reading of any Shakespearean play will
quickly reveal, but many of them have succumbed to the
pressure of the regular ending in *-ed*. A good example is *dive*
which retains its irregular preterite *dove* in American English,
but which is now *dived* in British English. Finally it may be
noted that a few verbs seem to combine the regular and
irregular ways of forming the preterite. The verb *to sleep* has
the preterite *slept*, in which the long vowel written *ee* has
been changed to the short vowel written *e*, and the regular
ending, which in this case is *-t* rather than *-ed*, has been
added.

   The present tense of all verbs has one variant form, the *-s*
form, which appears as *-es* after certain consonants, as in *he
lunches*. Traditionally this is said to be the form of the third
person singular of the present tense. It is singular because it
is found only when the subject of the sentence is singular and
the verb form agrees with it; thus we find *the boy walks*, but *the
boys walk*. When the subject is in the plural as in *boys*, the
verb retains the base form, which is without *-s*. It is third
person, because it is usual to divide personal pronouns into
three persons, and the corresponding verb forms are referred

to in the same way. The first person refers to the speaker or the *I* pronoun; the second person is the person spoken to or the *you* pronoun; and the third person is neither the speaker nor the person spoken to, and thus includes *he, she, it* and all other noun groups. These distinctions of person apply to both singular and plural. Since the verb form changes only in the third person singular of the present tense, the concept of person in the verb is not of much importance in modern English, but it can be represented schematically as follows:

singular	first	I walk
	second	you walk
	third	he(*etc*) walks
plural	first	we walk
	second	you walk
	third	they(*etc*) walk

However, there is one verb in which it still has some importance, in so far as the verb *to be* is so irregular that it has different forms for certain persons. The first person singular is *I am*, the third person singular is *he is*, and the second person singular and all the plural persons use *are*. The verb *to have* does have an *-s* form but it is different from what might have been expected since it is *has* rather than *haves*. Although the *-s* form of the third person singular of the present tense can be considered regular for all verbs, there are some exceptions. The principal exception is that verbs which can be used only as auxiliaries do not have an *-s* form. We have to say *He may come*; we cannot say *He mays come*. Those verbs such as *need* and *dare* which can be used as auxiliaries or as the head of a verb group have no *-s* in the former case, although they have one in the latter instance. Thus we find *He need not come* as against *He needs me*.

The verb in earlier English did have more endings in the present tense than is now the case, and they may still be encountered in certain varieties of the language. The older forms of the third person singular ended not in -*(e)s*, but in -*eth*. This may still be found in some archaic and literary varieties. Similarly, we used to have a second person singular pronoun *thou*, because *you* was originally only the second person plural pronoun. The present-tense ending which went with the *thou* pronoun was -*est* and produced examples such as *thou walkest*. This form may still occasionally be found in religious, particularly liturgical, varieties of English.

The preterite tense of the verb does not change at all in the various persons except in the case of the verb *to be*, which is once more an exception. In this verb the first and third persons singular have *was* (*I was* and *he was*) and the rest of the preterite has *were* forms. The second person singular took over the *were* form when the plural pronoun *you* was extended to the singular. In older varieties of the language it is possible to meet the *thou* pronoun as the second singular form. When that happens, the preterite has the form *wert*, though it must be said that this is very rare.

The last two forms of the verb which exhibit a change are those which are called the present participle and the past participle. The present participle is formed by adding -*ing* to the base form of verbs, whether they are regular or irregular. Thus we find *writing* and *walking*. No change of vowel is involved even in the irregular verbs. The form of the past participle depends on whether a verb is regular or irregular. The regular verbs have a past participle which is the same as the preterite tense and ends in -*ed* (or -*t* as the case may be). Thus *walked* is both the preterite and the past participle of the verb *to walk*. Irregular verbs have a variety of forms, though they often exhibit a change of the root vowel and the ending -*(e)n*. Thus *write* has the preterite *wrote* and the past participle *written*. Although the vowel of *written* looks in writing to be the same as *write*, the pronunciation makes it clear that the former is a short vowel and the latter a diphthong. Often the vowel of the past participle will be the same as that of the base form or of the preterite. Thus the past participle *shaken* has the same vowel as the base form *shake*, and *forgotten* has the same vowel as the preterite *forgot*. It will be seen that both the present and the past participles are used with auxiliaries to form what can be called expanded tenses and other forms of the verbs, and so it is better to delay a consideration of their meaning and use until we have considered the auxiliaries. It may be added that auxiliaries which have no -*s* form are also without a present or past participle.

Most verbs, then, have the possibility of five different forms when they act as the head of a verb group. These are the base form, the -*(e)s* form, the preterite, the present participle in -*ing*, and the past participle. The base form is the one which is used as the headword for a verb in a dictionary. If you want to find *wrote* in a dictionary, you would have to look it up under the headword *write*, for there will be no entry for *wrote*. In regular verbs the base remains unchanged in all cases, for other forms of the verb are created by the addition of various endings to the base. Not all verbs exhibit different forms. As we have seen, regular verbs have the same form for the preterite and the past participle, and so they have only four forms. Irregular verbs may also have fewer than five forms, though this is less common. For example, the verb *to cut* does not change its vowel or add an ending to form the preterite. *I cut* could refer either to the present or to the past. Some verbs have more than the five forms, among which is the verb *to be* with eight.

As auxiliaries present rather more problems than the extension, it is preferable to take the latter first. An extension consists of a word or words which are to be understood as part of the verb and modify its meaning so that a verb with its extension has a quite separate sense from the simple verb by itself. *To take off*, which may mean 'to get going sucessfully', is something quite different from *to take*. Extensions can take many forms, but two are common. The first is that of a prepositional adverb such as *off* or *up*, which is usually added to a common monosyllabic verb such as *take* or *set*. It is important to recognise when this word belongs to the verb group and when it is a preposition with its own following noun phrase. Usually the meaning will be a sufficient guide, but it is also possible to employ substitution of the verb group by another word or to rearrange the sentence order or structure. Consider the following two sentences:

1   He came round last night.
2   He came round the corner too fast.

Both contain the words *came round*. In the first example *round* is an extension to *came*, and the verb group may mean he 'paid a visit'. In the second *round* goes with *the corner* because it tells us where he came. The close link of *round* with *the corner* is indicated through the possibility of placing *too fast* between *came* and *round*; but it would not be allowable to break up the sequence of *round the corner* by putting *too fast* after *round*. It would, though, be possible to substitute for *round the corner* an adverb such as *there*. In the first example, if one were to substitute a verb group for *came round*, it would have to replace both *came* and *round*; it would not be possible to substitute something just for *came* and to leave *round* in the sentence. An expression that could be substituted for *came round* is *dropped in*.

The second common form of extension consists of those words which have come to form an idiomatic expression with the head of the verb group so that the whole has a completely separate meaning from that which is implied by its parts. When one says colloquially that *He kicked the bucket*, *the bucket* could be understood as a noun group which is the object of *kicked*. But the whole expression *kicked the bucket* may have nothing to do with kicking or with buckets; it may be another way of saying 'He died'. It is therefore quite reasonable to consider *kicked the bucket* in this usage as a verb group consisting of a head *kicked* and an extension *the bucket*. It is naturally impossible to characterise this type of extension since it occurs in many different forms. However, one can say that the extension of the verb group, unlike the qualifier in a noun group, consists of a formulaic set of words which cannot be expanded. One cannot say *He kicked the grey bucket* without changing the structure of the sentence, for *the grey bucket* would be a noun group acting as the object of *kicked* and not as the extension within the verb group. Each extension is usually no more than three words long, and the majority contain only a single word.

The auxiliaries fall into different categories of which the following are the principal ones. They can be distinguished partly by the auxiliary which is used and partly by the form which the head of the verb group takes with it. The best known are probably the MODAL auxiliaries. These include the following verbs: *will, shall, can, may*, with their past forms *would, should, could* and *might*; *must*, which has no separate past form; and *ought to, dare, need* and *used to*, which in their use resemble other verbs considered to be full auxiliaries. They are called modals because unlike other verbs they do not indicate an action, but rather they suggest a mood (hence *modal*) or attitude towards an action. Thus *He may hit him* does not mean that any action is performed, but only that an action is possible. With these modals one can also group the auxiliary *do*, which is known as a PERIPHRASTIC auxiliary. This is used in a sentence either for formal reasons, such as to create a question or a negative, or for emphasis. It is not a modal auxiliary, for when it is included the action indicated by the verb does take place. *He did hit him* indicates that the action *hit* occurred. The modals and the periphrastic auxiliary share two features: firstly, they always occupy the first position if there is more than one auxiliary before the head of the verb group; and, secondly, if they come immediately before the head then the head will be in the base form. As examples of the first feature consider *He will be coming tomorrow* and *He should have arrived yesterday* in which *will* and *should* come before *be* and *have*. In these cases, as the modal auxiliaries are separated from the head by another auxiliary, the head does not have the base form. As examples of the second feature consider *He will arrive tomorrow* and *He did lunch with me*, in which the heads have the base form because the modal or periphrastic auxiliary precedes it immediately. This rule still applies in questions and negative sentences: *Will he arrive tomorrow?* and *He did not lunch with me*. It is only if the modal auxiliary is separated by another auxiliary from the head that the head will have some form other than the base form. As a general rule periphrastic *do* is not used with other auxiliaries and so it is regularly followed by the base form.

The modals differ from the other auxiliaries in that they can be used only as auxiliaries: apart from *need* and *dare* they cannot appear as the head of a verb group except in those cases where the head is omitted through ellipsis, which is when some part of a sentence which is needed for the sense is omitted as it is understood from the context. Thus if one asks *Will he come tonight?*, the answer could be *He may*, in which *may* appears to act as the head of the verb group. However, *may* is here elliptical for *may come*, but *come* is omitted as it can be understood from the preceding question. The other main verbs which can act as auxiliaries are *be* and *have* as well as the periphrastic *do*, and these all function as the head of a verb group regularly as well. It is *have* and *be* which provide the other categories of auxiliary verbs. *Have*, which constitutes the second category, is followed by the head in the past participial form and it is known as the PERFECTIVE auxiliary. Examples are *He has eaten his breakfast* and *He had been to the bank*. In each case *has* or *had* is followed by the past participle *eaten* or *been*. Both of these examples refer to actions which took place in the past, and it is important to distinguish them from the preterite tense. In discussing the basic forms that a verb can take we saw that the base form, which provides the present tense, could be changed either through the addition of *-ed* or the change of the root vowel to give the preterite. This tense is used of an action which is complete and has no bearing on what is happening or being said in the present. When *have* in the present tense is used as an auxiliary with the head in the past participle form, it is said to constitute the PERFECT form of the verb. Although this also refers to an action in the past, that action is thought to have relevance to or a bearing on what is happening in the present. This difference may be illustrated by the following sentences: *Jane was ill for a week* and *Jane has been ill for a week*. In the first example it is implied through the preterite form *was* that although Jane was ill for a week, she is now better; whereas in the second example it would be assumed from the perfect form *has been* that not only had Jane been ill for a week, but she was still ill at that moment. When the preterite of *have* is used as an auxiliary with the head in the past participle, it is said to produce the PLUPERFECT form, and this usually refers to a period of time which precedes the past time which is otherwise the subject of discussion. In *After Jane had been ill for a week, they sent for the doctor*, the time represented by *had been* is earlier than the time represented by *sent*, though both refer to times in the past. Since *have* is used to produce these perfect and pluperfect forms, it is not difficult to understand why it is referred to as a perfective auxiliary. The perfective auxiliary follows the modals and precedes the other auxiliaries in the order of the verb group. In *He may have arrived*, the *have* follows the modal *may*; and in *He may have been sent home* it follows *may* but precedes *been*.

The other two categories of auxiliary are formed with *be* and they differ simply in the form taken by the head which follows. In the third category the auxiliary is followed by the present participle; and in the fourth it is followed by the past participle. When the auxiliary *be* is followed by the present participle it is known as the PROGRESSIVE, for it refers to an action which is in progress at the time referred to. *Jane is living in London* means that she is living there at the moment, but does not habitually do so. This progressive form is often thought to constitute one of the three varieties of the present tense, the differences among which are so characteristic of English and cause so many problems for foreign speakers. These three varieties are the present tense proper, which uses the base or -*s* form of the verb, the form consisting of periphrastic auxiliary *do* and the base of the head, and that consisting of the *be* auxiliary and the present participle of the head. Examples are *he lives, he does live* and *he is living*. The *be* with present participle comes after the *have* auxiliary and before the *be* with past participle in the order of the verb group.

The final category of auxiliary is *be* with the past participle, which produces the verb form known as the PASSIVE. The concept of the passive is one which will need to be discussed in greater detail later, but its main characteristics need to be touched on briefly here. The three previous categories of auxiliary are characterised as the active, as distinct from the passive, part of the verb in so far as in the active verb the subject does the action and in the passive the subject suffers the action which is represented by the verb. Consider the following examples:

1 Dorinda sent the parcel.
2 Dorinda may send the parcel.

3   Dorinda has sent the parcel.
4   Dorinda is sending the parcel.
5   Dorinda was sent to London.

In the first four cases (one with a simple verb and three with auxiliaries) Dorinda is doing the sending: she is causing the parcel to be sent. In the fifth example it is Dorinda herself who is being sent; she is not doing the sending. The passive is always formed by a part of *be* acting as an auxiliary and the past participle. This auxiliary can be used with other auxiliaries, and when it is it will always take the final position in the sequence of auxiliaries. If it does occur, it will always make the sentence passive so that the subject suffers the action of the verb, no matter how many other auxiliaries there may be. This can be shown by the example *Dorinda should have been being questioned by the headmaster*, which also illustrates some of the other features discussed earlier. In this example it is Dorinda who is to be questioned, and the headmaster who will do the questioning. Dorinda as subject suffers the action of the verb and so the sentence is passive. The sentence also reveals that the auxiliaries have to occur in a particular order: first the modal *should*, then the *have* auxiliary, and finally the two *be* auxiliaries. When a modal auxiliary is followed by the head, that goes in the base form; but if the head does not follow immediately then the following auxiliary takes the base form instead; so the modal *should* is followed by the *have* auxiliary in its base form *have*. Similarly the *have* auxiliary is followed by the head in the past participial form; but if the head does not follow immediately then the next auxiliary takes the past participial form instead; so the *have* auxiliary is followed by the *be* auxiliary in its past participial form *been*. The *be* progressive auxiliary is followed by the present participial form; and so it is followed in this sentence by *being* which is the *-ing* participle. Finally the passive auxiliary is followed by the head in the past participial form; so *being* is followed by *questioned*, which is the past participle of the head *question*.

Verb groups with four auxiliaries are not common in English, though writers who wish to give an impression of weight may often use more auxiliaries than are strictly necessary. As I have indicated, the number of auxiliaries is very restricted, and they have to appear in the verb group in a prescribed order. The scope for variety is small. Equally the extensions of the verb group fall into certain patterns, which cannot easily be modified or expanded. This is a matter of some importance because it is in this respect quite different from the noun group, which can be expanded almost indefinitely. This means that in practice the elaboration which writers wish to build into their style is more likely to be concentrated in the noun than in the verb group because of the restrictions which hedge in the latter. The use of too many verb groups with auxiliaries can only create a heavy and pretentious style rather than an expansive or metaphorical one. As verbs indicate action, language which is dynamic may well rely on a higher proportion of verbs. In such cases it is most likely that the verb groups will consist of only a head in either the present or the preterite tense.

In addition to the structure of the verb group, it is possible to think of the verb as falling into other categories. As we saw, the verb may be defined as the word which indicates the action carried out by the subject. One type of sentence in modern English has no subject and that is the sentence which contains an order or command. The verbs of such sentences are said to be in the IMPERATIVE. When we order someone to do something, we say something like *Come here* or *Sit down*. There is no subject pronoun *you* in such sentences, though that can be found in earlier varieties of English. The imperative occurs only in the base form. This corresponds to the present tense, though there is naturally no -*s* form because commands are always to be understood as implying the second person as they are addressed directly to the listener or listeners. An imperative in the third person is not possible, though one in the first person is if the speaker includes himself in the command, as he does in an imperative such as *Let's go home*. Even in this instance there is no subject pronoun. The imperative part of the verb can be differentiated from other verb forms simply through the absence of a noun group acting as subject. It is true that some utterances may be understood as commands even though they do not have the imperative forms. If I say to my students *Will you please hand in your essays tomorrow?*, they will doubtless understand that to be an order. But the sentence is actually formulated as a question and the verb must not be taken as an imperative.

In modern English we distinguish a statement of fact from statements of possibility or intention through the use of modal auxiliaries. *He came* states a fact, but with the modal auxiliary *might* in *He might come* we have only the possibility of intention indicated. In older varieties of English, when auxiliaries were less developed, it was necessary to express this type of possible action through changes to the base form of the verb. Verbs in such cases were said to be in the SUBJUNCTIVE. The subjunctive has largely disappeared from contemporary English, but as there are still one or two survivals of it we must refer to it briefly. The indicative of the verb, which is essentially all that survives today in the forms of the base, *-s* and preterite, indicates a fact, whereas the subjunctive indicates something which at the moment of speaking is either hypothetical or not known to be a fact. A wish is a good example of something which at the time of its utterance is clearly not a fact; and it is in the expression of wishes that the old subjunctive form still remains. The present tense of verbs has only one form which varies from the base and that is the *-s* form of the third person singular. The subjunctive is now only to be recognised in those cases where no *-s* is found in the third person singular. We still say *Long live the queen* rather than *Long may the queen live* with an auxiliary. The first of those two sentences has the subjunctive *live* rather than the indicative *lives* because it expresses a wish rather than a fact. Sentences such as *Long live the queen* have survived because they are formulaic; most other wishes are now expressed through an auxiliary or, more frequently, through the addition at the beginning of the wish of something like *I hope that*. The subjunctive may still, though now very rarely, be found in clauses beginning with an *if*, which must indicate something which is not a fact. Although it is possible to say *If he come tonight, tell him*, this sentence is more likely to be expressed as *If he comes tonight, tell him*. The verb *to be* is again exceptional in preserving some subjunctive forms. Many people still say *If I were you, I'd tell him*, in which *were* is the subjunctive indicating something which is hypothetical as compared with the indicative *was*.

There are, as we saw earlier, five forms of most verbs, and these can be divided into FINITE and NON-FINITE categories. The former are those which can act by themselves as a complete verb group, whereas the latter must have some other element such as an auxiliary in the verb group. The finite forms are the base, the -*s* form, and the preterite, and these when used by themselves will make a complete verb group. The non-finite forms are the present and past participles. These cannot act as complete verb groups by themselves and a sentence will not be well-formed if the verb group consists only of a non-finite part of a verb. *She seeing him* does not make an acceptable sentence, for the present participle needs an auxiliary if it is to act as the verb of a sentence. *She was seeing him* would make an acceptable sentence. However, the non-finite parts of the verb can act as modifiers or qualifiers in a noun group, and this is a role which is not available to the finite parts. It is perfectly possible to have noun groups such as *the ruined city* or *the deepening crisis*, in which *ruined* and *deepening* are past and present participles acting as modifiers.

A verb such as *steal* can operate in two distinct ways. as can be seen by considering the following two sentences:

1 Dorinda stole an apple.
2 Dorinda stole away.

In each sentence *Dorinda* is the subject. But in the first sentence the verb *stole* has an object, indicating that which was stolen. In the second sentence there is no object, because *away* is the extension of the verb group and there is nothing which was stolen away. When a verb takes an object it is said to be TRANSITIVE, and when it does not it is said to be INTRANSITIVE. Some verbs may be used either transitively or intransitively, though it is more usual for a verb to be either one or the other. Thus a verb such as *hit* is always transitive for it will always be used with an object, the person or thing which is hit; but *die* on the other hand is intransitive because at present it is not possible to construct a sentence in which *die* has an object. Verbs which indicate motion, such as *arrive*, *come* and *go*, are intransitive. Two types of verb are neither transitive nor intransitive, for although they have an 'object' which follows the verb it is one which refers back to the subject. Although they have something which resembles an object, these verbs are otherwise more like intransitives. Consider the following three sentences:

1   The boy loves the girl.
2   The boy is a prince.
3   The boy behaved himself

In the first sentence the object *girl* is quite different from the subject *boy*; two separate people are involved. But in the second and third sentences this is not the case. It is the boy who is a prince, and so *prince* and *boy* refer to the same person. This type of object is known in traditional grammar as a COMPLEMENT. This complement may be a noun or an adjective, as can be seen in

1   The boy is a prince.
2   The boy is unhappy.

In the sentence *The boy behaved himself*, the 'object' is a reflexive pronoun which refers back to the subject: the *him* of *himself* means the boy. Verbs which take a reflexive pronoun are sometimes known as reflexive verbs. It is a feature of modern English that reflexive verbs are gradually dying out of the language. This is happening through the omission of the reflexive pronoun, so transforming the reflexive verb into an intransitive one. Instead of saying *The boy behaved himself*, it is perfectly possible to say *The boy behaved*; and in some sentences, such as *Can't you ever behave sensibly?*, it is now relatively rare to find the reflexive pronoun *yourself*.

It is important to remember the distinction between transitive and intransitive verbs because it has a bearing on the formation of the passive. It was pointed out above that verbs could have a passive as well as an active form. All verbs have an active, for the base is always the active form. The passive is formed from the active through the use of the *be* auxiliary and by making the object of the active sentence into the subject of the passive sentence, so that *The boy hit the man* becomes *The man was hit by the boy.* Since the formation of the passive involves the transformation of the object into the subject, it follows that only transitive verbs can have a passive. Verbs with a complement or which take a reflexive pronoun are like intransitive verbs in that they do not have a true object which can be turned into a subject. There can be no passive forms of *Dorinda stole away*, *The boy is a prince*, *The boy is unhappy* and *The boy behaved himself.* There are two advantages which accrue from the use of the passive. The first is that it focuses attention on what is actually the object of the action by making it the subject of the passive verb. It achieves this because the subject in an English sentence comes at the beginning. Since English has developed a rather inflexible word order, the principal way in which the real object of a verb can be placed near the beginning of the sentence is through the use of the passive. The passive has expanded its role through the history of English as the word order became more rigid, and it provides one of the compensations for that word order. The second is that the real subject of the verb need not be expressed. It can be indicated through the use of a preposition such as *by* as we saw in the example earlier in this paragraph. However, the agent who is performing the action of the verb and who would form the subject of an active verb need not be specifically mentioned in a passive sentence so that *The man was hit by the boy* could be simply *The man was hit.* The *by the boy* is not needed to make an acceptable English sentence. The suppression of the agent is not uncommon in notices, because a notice may give the impression of greater authority when the person issuing it is not mentioned directly. If you receive a form which says *You are required to return this form within thirty days*, the absence of any indication as to who is enforcing this requirement makes the instruction more universal and authoritative. Similarly, in books about language such as this one, the rules about language which are mentioned may be put into the passive form because that allows the author to avoid saying whether he has made the rule up himself or, if not, who precisely it is who has said that it is a rule.

Earlier in the chapter two features of English verbs were mentioned in reference to the present tense: namely, that, in addition to the base form *come*, verbs could also in the present tense have a progressive form *is coming* and a periphrastic *do* form *does come*. In fact not all verbs can have these three forms, for, although all verbs have a base form, some cannot have the progressive or the periphrastic forms. The sentence *She comes every day* can be changed into *She is coming every day* and *She does come every day*; but the sentence *She is a student* cannot be changed into *She is being a student* or into *She does be a student*. Verbs which cannot make these additional forms are known as STATIVE, because they indicate a state rather than an action. Those verbs which can have these forms are known as DYNAMIC. It is possible to turn a stative into a dynamic verb for certain purposes. This is true even of the verb *to be* in an example such as *She was being good when he arrived*. Because of this it may be better, as with transitive and intransitive, to think of stative and dynamic uses of verbs.

Verbs refer to actions or, in the case of stative verbs, imply a state. Both actions and states are not confined to a single moment of time, and so verbs may have a much more diffuse reference than nouns. In a novel you might easily come across such a sentence as *John returned home and went to bed*. The actions implied here are numerous and long drawn out. If John was a long way from his home to start with, he would perhaps have had to get his car and drive it back to his house. He would at the very least have had to get into his house and get undressed before he went to bed. From the point of view of this particular novelist the precise stages of going home and getting to bed are unimportant, though it would be possible to focus on one or more of them if necessary. The focus that can be applied to a verb is known as ASPECT. The two major forms of aspect are the progressive and non-progressive on the one hand, and the perfective and non-perfective on the other. The non-progressive indicates indefinite time or habitual activity as compared with the temporary nature of the progressive. *Dorinda peels the potatoes* indicates something which is habitual, but *Dorinda is peeling the potatoes* something which is happening on a particular occasion only. With past time the difference is one of completeness or not. In the sentence *Dorinda peeled the potatoes*, the activity would be understood as completed, whereas *Dorinda was peeling the potatoes* implies that this particular job was not finished in relation to any subsequent action. With perfective and non-perfective aspect the difference is one of relevance to the time of utterance: perfective aspect still has some relevance to the time of the rest of the utterance, whereas non-perfective aspect does not. *Dorinda has lived in Sheffield for a year* implies that she is still living there and it is the immediately preceding year in which she has been in Sheffield. On the other hand, *Dorinda lived in Sheffield for a year* has no such implication. The year will be understood as being some time in the past.

There are other features of aspect. If we recall the example at the beginning of the last paragraph, *John returned home and went to bed*, the two verbs indicate actions and it is possible to focus on the actions as a whole or on the beginning or end of each of them. Actions can be either habitual or once only; but they can also be repeated. In the sentence *John hit him*, the *hit* may mean once or it could mean several times. Generally these other features of aspect, such as a repeated action, do not affect the grammar of English in that they do not involve the use of auxiliaries or different verb forms.

In many ways the verb group is simpler than the noun group because it has fewer parts and cannot be expanded indefinitely. It tends, therefore, to be paid less attention in studies of style. In grammatical terms it may well seem more complicated and important than the noun because the verb itself has so many different features, such as the pairs transitive/intransitive, progressive/non-progressive and stative/dynamic. The proper distinction between these pairs can cause difficulties to non-native speakers of the language. The verb is not nearly so easy to understand as it may appear at first sight.

4   The Other Classes

The word classes which have not been dealt with in the previous two chapters are adverbs, conjunctions, prepositions and interjections. Of these the adverb is probably the most important, and certainly the most difficult. Its importance reflects the fact that it is the only one of these remaining classes which belongs to the open category of words and which can act as an independent unit within the structure of a sentence. Its difficulty springs from the heterogeneous nature of the adverb and from the similarity in function which many adverbs have to words in other classes. Perhaps we may consider this latter difficulty first.

The most common formal characteristic of an adverb is that it has the ending *-ly*. This ending is one which has been increasingly attached to adverbs since the seventeenth century, partly as a means to distinguish them from adjectives. Without the *-ly* ending there is no difference in form between an adjective and an adverb, as can still be seen from those words which occur so frequently that they have never adopted the ending. Examples are *fast* and *late*. With words of this type it may sometimes be difficult to decide whether a particular example is an adjective or an adverb. From the parallel of *The boy is happy*, where *happy* is an adjective, in *The train is late* it is tempting to analyse *late* as an adjective as well. Although *happy* clearly describes *boy* and it is possible to rephrase the expression as *the happy boy*, *late* does not describe the *train* as such, but rather its progress. It is not possible to rephrase the statement as *the late train*, which means something quite different. Hence *late* is an adverb in this sentence, and is equivalent in function to *there* in *The train is there*. Although it is possible to come to a conclusion about the status of *late*, it is not so easy with some other words. Those which begin with *a*- are particularly troublesome; they include such words as *abroad* and *asleep*. Grammarians have varied as to their allocation of these words to the adjective or adverb class, and it may be that in some senses they are adverbs and in other adjectives. You might like to think of sentences in which these words are acceptable and others in which they are not. Although we accept *The man is asleep* and *The man seemed asleep*, we do not normally allow *The man travelled asleep*.

In the last chapter we saw that the extension of the verb group could be formed by a prepositional adverb. The name implies that the word is usually a preposition, but may on occasion change its function to that of adverb. In *She set up the display units*, *up* goes with the verb *set* and can be interpreted as the extension in the verb group. While some of these extensions must be placed next to the head of the verb group, others may be separated from it. In *She laid down the law*, *down* cannot be moved to a different position in the sentence; but in *She ate up her dinner*, it is perfectly permissible to rewrite this as *She ate her dinner up*. When, as in this last example, the extension is separated from the head of the verb group, it is difficult to decide whether one should treat it as an adverb or continue regarding it as the extension in a verb group. In this case *up* has an adverbial sense implying 'entirely, completely', and it is possible to omit it altogether, since *She ate her dinner* makes good sense. Prepositions normally come before a noun or noun group, and when this is not the case they cease essentially to be prepositions and are transformed into adverbs. It is as adverbs that they become joined to verbs as extensions of the verb group. Naturally enough in view of the development of these forms, it is not always easy to decide into which class a particular word fits: whether the adverb has definitely become an extension or not.

Some adverbs, as we shall see in a moment, can stand outside the main structure of a sentence because they act as a comment on the whole of the sentence. The sentence is complete without the adverb, which simply adds some emotional overtone to the utterance. Thus *He's just gone home* is a well-formed sentence to which various adverbs can be added to give some colouring to the statement. These could include *Actually he's just gone home* or *Truly he's just gone home.* This function of adding some emotional colouring to a sentence is also accomplished by interjections. Our example could be varied to *Damn, he's just gone home.* That modern vogue expression *you know* is another item that could be added to the sentence for the same reason: *He's just gone home, you know.* The adverb which adds this kind of comment to a sentence is consequently fulfilling the same function as an expletive, though the words which are thought of as expletives occupy a different range of acceptability from adverbs for most speakers of the language. It is also true that some interjections have a slightly different function from these adverbs and show other peculiarities, as we shall see, which suggest that they should be kept apart as a separate category.

Finally, adverbs have points of contact with conjunctions. The function of a conjunction is to link two clauses together. In the sentence *After he put the cat out, she went to bed, after* acts as a linking work which binds the two actions (putting out the cat, and going to bed) in a temporal relationship. One action follows the other in time. If, however, one rewrote this as *He put the cat out; then she went to bed,* it could be said that *then* is fulfilling the same function as *after* since it is linking the two clauses together in the same temporal relationship. There is a formal difference between these two utterances in that *After he put the cat out, she went to bed* forms a single sentence, whereas *He put the cat out; then she went to bed* is made up of two units each of which could stand independently, as is indicated by the semi-colon. This is true and points up a difference between *then* and *after.* On the other hand, there are conjunctions which join two independent units together. Our example could be rewritten as *He put the cat and she went to bed;* and this example consists of two clauses which could each stand independently in much the same way as the sentence with *then.* But *and* is considered to be a conjunction and *then* an adverb. The link between conjunctions of this type and adverbs is even closer when the former stands at the head of the sentence, as is true of the previous sentence, where *but* is the opening word. In older prescriptive grammars a common rule was that no sentence should begin with *and* or *but*, precisely because these were considered to be only conjunctions whose function was to join two clauses, phrases or words together. A conjunction which came at the beginning of a sentence was clearly not accomplishing any of those functions and so, it was argued, it could not be placed there. This rule ignores the fact that almost everybody does begin sentences with *but* and *and*, and examples can readily be found in this book. When they are in the initial position in a sentence, conjunctions such as *and* and *but* are no different in function from such adverbs as *then*; it is still customary to refer to them as conjunctions despite this similarity with the adverbial function. From what has been written so far it is apparent that the adverb has many points of contact with a number of other word classes.

The adverb can act as a independent unit of a sentence. We can divide the parts of the sentence *The train arrived late* into *The train*, subject (noun group); *arrived*, verb (verb group); and *late*, adverb. The adverb is of the same status as the subject and verb within the sentence, and just as the subject and verb are said to be formed of a noun group and verb group respectively, so also it is reasonable to accept that the adverb can be formed of an adverb group. This means that the adverb function in a sentence can be achieved through more than one word, just as the subject through the noun group can be represented by one or more words. The previous example could easily be rewritten *The train arrived after lunch* or *The train arrived in a snowstorm*, in which *after lunch* and *in a snowstorm* occupy the same role as *late*. Many adverbs which are single words formed from adjectives can also be modified by an intensifier, so that the first example in this paragraph could be rephrased *The train arrived very late*.

The examples in the previous paragraph illustrate the diverse nature of the adverb group. With the noun group and the verb group it is possible to outline a structure which all noun groups and all verb groups adhere to. Each has a head, and that head can be preceded and followed by certain restricted types of word. The adverb group is different. It can consist of a single word, which would be traditionally labelled an adverb. That adverb may itself be modified by an intensifier. Alternatively an adverb group may consist of a preposition and its accompanying noun phrase, such as *after lunch* and *in a snowstorm*. Although *after lunch* and *late* fulfil the same function in the sentence, since each can be substituted for the other, as individual words they are very different, since one consists of a preposition and a noun and the other of an adverb. It is of course possible to have a noun phrase by itself acting as an adverb group. Our sentence could be rewritten *The train arrived this morning*, in which *this morning* fulfils the same function as *late* and *after lunch*. The adverb group is therefore very different from the noun and verb group, for it is heterogeneous in its make-up whereas they have a regular structure. It is partly for this reason that it is so difficult to characterise the adverb group or even for that matter the adverb itself. In some ways it may be helpful to think of it as the category which contains anything left over in the sentence when all the other main constituents have been analysed. After the subject, verb, complement and object(s) have been identified in a sentence, anything which has still not been analysed is likely to be an adverb or adverb group. This is a rather negative approach, and it is better to provide some outline of the functions the adverb or adverb group can carry out.

In the discussion of the noun group we saw that adverbs could act as intensifiers to modifiers and thus represents the first function of an adverb. When an adverb acts as an intensifer, and it is not only modifiers which can be intensified, it does not function as an adverb group in itself, but it is part of another group, which may be either a noun group or an adverb group. In *a very happy boy*, *very* is an adverb acting as an intensifier to the modifier of a noun group; the adverb is an integral part of the noun group. In *very fortunately*, *very* is an adverb acting as an intensifier to another adverb and together they form an adverb group. In this instance two adverbs go to form an adverb group; and one can think of *fortunately* as the head of that group and *very* as its intensifier. Since an adverb can be modified by an intensifier and since intensifiers are adverbs, it is possible to have one intensifier modified by a second one. In *That's a much more convincing answer*, *more* is an intensifer of *convincing*, but *much* is an intensifier of *more*. This sentence could be expanded to *That's a very much more convincing answer*, in which there are three intensifiers, each intensifying the word which follows. It is, however, not only adjectives and adverbs which can be modified by intensifiers. Within the noun group it is possible also to intensify a determiner and a pre-determiner, though the former is not very common. In *He's been here for almost a week*, *almost* intensifies *a*, which here reveals its origin as a weakened form of *one*, since the sense is 'almost the whole of one week'. *Almost* can also be used to intensify pre-determiners as in *Almost half the students failed to complete the exam*, in which *almost* intensifies *half*. In colloquial English intensifiers can be applied directly to nouns. In *It was some party*, *some* is an intensifier to *party*; but this usage is not found in standard written English. Prepositions also can be modified by intensifiers. In *She kissed him right on the nose*, *right* is an intensifier to the preposition *on*. Naturally in colloquial English there is a far wider range of intensifiers and the previous example might have been expressed colloquially as *She kissed him bang on the nose*. The aim of an intensifier is, as its name suggests, to sharpen the meaning of the word which it modifies. Since colloquial language goes in for more colourful expression, it is not surprising that intensifiers are found more commonly in speech, and that the words which can be used as intensifiers are more numerous.

An adverb can also be found in one or two unexpected positions. In discussing the structure of the noun group in a previous chapter we noticed that the qualifier could in certain circumstances consist of a single word. One of those is when that word is an adverb. *Above* in the sentence *The output of English steel mills can be consulted in the table above* forms the qualifier of the noun group *the table above*. Many native speakers understand this noun group as elliptical for *the table which is given above*, in which the adverbial nature of *above* is much clearer. It may well be because English speakers still think of *above* as an adverb in examples such as this one that it remains generally unacceptable to rephrase the noun phrase by putting *above* as a modifier to give *the above table*. The other position where the adverb occurs rather unexpectedly is after a preposition, since the common definition of a preposition is that it is placed before a noun. The word *above* is an adverb and not a noun, and yet it can follow a preposition as in *The light shone down from above*. Such examples indicate that the definition of a preposition should be expanded to allow for this possibility by indicating that it is a word that occurs usually before a noun, but sometimes before other word classes.

The commonest use of the adverb or adverb group is not only to be part of the sentence structure at the same level as subject and verb, but also to be closely integrated into that structure. The adverb differs from the subject and verb in that its position in the sentence is freer. An adverb can be placed at the beginning or end of a clause and at various positions within it. The less free an adverb is as regards its position, the more closely integrated into the structure of a sentence it is. There are certain tests which can be applied to determine whether an adverb belongs to the common type under discussion or not. The freedom of movement of an adverb can be illustrated by *He walked home slowly*, for *slowly* can be moved to the other positions in the sentence, particularly the beginning to give *Slowly he walked home*. The first test is to make the sentence negative, for in negative sentences this type of adverb cannot be placed at the beginning. We cannot say *Slowly he did not walk home*. The second test is whether the adverb can be put in a sentence, particularly an interrogative or a negative one, so that it forms a contrast with its opposite. *He walked home slowly* could be altered in this way to *Did he walk home slowly or quickly?* or to *He didn't walk home slowly; he walked quickly*. In both these latter sentences *slowly* is set in contrast with *quickly*. These tests apply whether one is dealing with an adverb group or an adverb. If the example above had been *He walked home in the morning*, the tests would show that one could not have *In the morning he did not walk home*, but that one could say *Did he walk home in the morning or after lunch?*

Adverbs can also be used which stand outside the basic structure of the sentence, and these react to the tests outlined in the previous paragraph in completely the opposite way. An adverb such as *actually* could be included in the example instead of *slowly* to give either *Actually he walked home* or *He walked home actually*. This word may be used at the beginning of the sentence even if it is negative: *Actually, he didn't walk home*. It may not be set in a contrastive relationship with another adverb: one cannot say *He didn't walk home actually, but he did frankly*. Adverbs of this type fall into two categories, which are in more modern grammars known as DISJUNCTS and CONJUNCTS. A disjuct adds some emotional colouring to the sentence to which it is attached and has no specific link with the sentences which precede and follow. A conjunct, on the other hand, is a linking adverb which involves a mechanism to provide some relationship between one sentence and the next. Consider the following examples:

1 First the plane was delayed for two hours. Then the flight was cancelled and he came home.
2 The plane was delayed for two hours. Luckily, he was able to get on a different flight.

In the first example there is a clear time relationship set up between the two sentences, and the two disjuncts, *first* and *then*, are the means whereby that relationship is made explicit. In the second example, *luckily* refers only to the information contained in the second sentence, for a delay is not normally thought of as lucky, though there is a general continuity between the two sentences, as there is in any utterance. It is much easier to delete *luckily* in the second example than it is *first* and *then* in the first, because each is required to make the link between the two sentences unambiguous. Without them, it would be uncertain when the flight was cancelled, for example. One-word disjuncts and conjuncts can be replaced by phrases forming an adverb group. *Briefly this is my plan* could be expressed as *In a nutshell this is my plan*; and in the first example above *then* could be replaced by *After all that time*.

Prepositions have already been the subject of comment at several places in the preceding chapters. The reason for this is that, unlike the other word classes we have considered, prepositions are not major sentence elements which can stand by themselves; they can only occur with other words to form a sentence element. A preposition such as *at* cannot by itself be the subject, object or verb of a sentence; it has to be linked with other words to fill this role. Words which are nouns, adjectives, verbs and adverbs are called lexical words – that is, words which have full meaning in themselves – whereas prepositions and conjunctions are called grammatical words, whose principal function is to express grammatical relationships between other words or groups in a sentence. It is because they express this relationship between words in other classes that they do not form sentence elements on their own. A preposition normally comes before a noun phrase, though it occasionally occurs before words of other classes, and together with these words it forms a prepositional phrase. A prepositional phrase, therefore, may be said to consist of a preposition and a completive, which in turn will normally be a noun phrase, but may sometimes be a word or words in another class. A prepositional phrase may either be the only member of a group such as an adverb group or it may be one of several constituent members of a group such as a noun group. This is a matter which we shall return to in the following chapter.

A prepositional phrase consists of a preposition and its completive, and in the phrase the preposition will normally come first. It is, however, possible for the preposition to come after the completive and to be separated from it. This happens particularly in questions and in relative clauses which form the qualifier of a noun group. In the latter case the relative pronoun is often omitted through ellipsis so that the preposition is left by itself. *What do you want to do that for?* provides an example of a question with the preposition at the end of the sentence. Here *for* is the preposition relating to *what*, which is its completive, and together they form a prepositional phrase. An example of the separation of preposition and its completive in a relative clause is provided by *The house which my aunt died in has just been sold*. Here the preposition *in* comes at the end of the clause and *which* comes at its beginning; but *which* is the completive of *in*. However, it must be said that the *which* in this type of clause is almost always omitted in speech and frequently even in writing, so that this sentence would often appear as *The house my aunt died in has just been sold*. This example has a bearing on the point made earlier about the close relationship between prepositions and adverbs. For when the completive of a prepositional phrase is elided in this way it leaves the preposition by itself so that it virtually takes on the status of an adverb, though the presence of the rest of the relative clause perhaps prevents that final transfer from the one class to the other. The presence of the rest of the relative clause makes this type of sentence different from the kind in which the completive of a prepositional phrase, which is a noun phrase, is omitted. In the dialogue

'Here's the park.'
'Let's go in.'

it would be possible to understand the final *in* as a preposition in a prepositional phrase *in the park*. But as *the park* is not expressed, *in* becomes an adverb which is no different from other adverbs which could appear in a similar position, such as *inside*. These two examples are treated rather differently by grammarians. In a relative clause such as *The house my aunt died in has just been sold* it still retains enough feel that the completive has been deleted for many to accept that *in* is here a preposition, whereas in *Let's go in* it is more usually understood to be an adverb.

When a preposition is followed by a pronoun as its completive, the pronoun will not be in the subject case in standard written English. We do not say *Give it to I*, because prepositions such as *to* must be followed by pronouns in the non-subject case; this example would have to be *Give it to me*. However, because of ellipsis in some sentences, this distinction has become somewhat blurred, particularly as it affects the relationship between prepositions and conjunctions. Conjunctions normally join two clauses together and so a conjunction will normally be followed by a pronoun in he subject case, for that will be acting as the subject of the following clause. In *He's taller than I am*, *than* is a conjunction followed by *I* in the subject case. With ellipsis, however, it is common to omit *am* in this sentence leaving it as *He's taller than I*, which is in its turn more often transformed into *He's taller than me*. The last form *He's taller than me* has been influenced by our understanding as speakers of the language that prepositions are followed by a pronoun in a non-subject case and that *than* has to be understood as a preposition since it is followed only be a pronoun and not by a clause. It is prepositions which are followed by pronouns as their completive, for conjunctions introduce clauses. Examples such as this caused considerable confusion to prescriptive grammarians, who tried to insist on *He's taller than I* as correct on the principle that *than* is a conjunction. But we perhaps have to accept that elision has turned it into a preposition, just as some prepositions have been turned into adverbs.

In traditional grammar it is customary to break down a sentence into its individual words and allocate each word to a particular word class. Prepositions are somewhat different in so far as prepositions can consist of two or three words as well as a single word. It is possible to divide them into complex and simple prepositions. In addition to the many simple prepositions such as *at*, *by*, *in* and *to*, there are complex ones such as *according to*, *instead of* and *in comparison with*. With two-word complex prepositions, the first word is an adverb, adjective or conjunction and the second is a simple preposition. In *because of* we have a conjunction *because* and the simple preposition *of*. It is not possible to separate these two words, for they function jointly as a single entity. In *She left him because of his cruelty*, it is not possible to let *because* or *of* stand alone. With three-word complex prepositions the commonest organisation is preposition + noun + preposition, as in *on account of*. In principle a three-word preposition is indivisible both syntactically and semantically. The example *on account of* makes sense as a complete unit and that sense would not be conveyed by its individual parts. Equally this complex preposition is a syntactic unit in that the noun cannot be changed in form. *On account of* cannot be altered to *on accounts of* (with the noun in the plural) or to *on the account of* (with a determiner before the noun). However, some of these prepositions do exhibit some variety syntatically; *in face of* can also appear as *in the face of*. Since a three-word complex preposition consists of preposition + noun + preposition, which is a not uncommon structure in English, it may be difficult to decide whether one is dealing with a complex preposition or a part of a noun phrase. In *she stood in front of the door*, we would understand *in front of* as a preposition; but in *She sat in the front of the car*, we would take *in the front of* as part of the adverb group *in the front of the car*, with *front* being the head of the noun phrase which forms the completive to the preposition *in*. It is apparent from these two examples that the boundary between the complex preposition and the noun phrase may sometimes be blurred.

There are some words which act like prepositions, but which are closely related to other word classes. For example, in *Following the meeting he went to dinner*, *following*, which is a present participle of the verb *to follow*, seems to be acting in the same way as a preposition, and indeed it could easily be replaced by the preposition *after*. There are many participial forms, both past and present, which can act in the same way. In *Given the time available, we'll have to fly*, *given* is a past participle which acts like a preposition. It could be replaced by the complex preposition *in view of*. Words of this type are best taken as prepositions.

Prepositions occur as part of a prepositional phrase. Prepositional phrases occur most commonly as qualifiers of a noun group or as adverb groups. They can fulfil the role of any type of adverb. They can also act as a qualifier of an adjective. In *He is happy in his job*, the *in his job* acts as a kind of qualifier to the adjective *happy*. Simple and complex prepositions can express a variety of different relations among lexical words in a sentence. The commonest meaning implied, particularly by simple prepositions, is that involving time or space. Complex prepositions tend to imply a rather more sophisticated relationship, such as cause and effect. It may be thought that *in view of* and *in comparison with* imply more complicated relationships than *in* or *to*. However, not all complex prepositions have this wider range of meaning.

Where a preposition expresses a relationship between two words, a conjunction expresses a similar relationship between two clauses, each of which will consist at least of its own subject and verb. In colloquial language it is common not to include a conjunction, so that the relationship between the two clauses must be inferred from the context. In *Look out, he's coming* the listener would readily understand that the *he* was a person of some authority who might not approve of whatever the listener was engaged in. In written language a conjunction such as *because* might well be added to make this relationship explicit. In older forms of written English the omission of conjunctions was frequent, and it is also now found in those types of written English which attempt to create a more colloquial style. Conjunctions expressing either causal or temporal relationships are the ones most likely to be omitted. It is also possible to insert a clause in parenthesis without relating it to the structure of the principal clause in order to add some emotional or other implication. This can be shown in the following sentence: *She loved him – how she loved him! – for many years without any reciprocation on his part.* In such sentences the clause in parenthesis fulfils the function of an interjection or disjunct, for it adds emotional emphasis to the main part of the sentence.

It is normal to divide conjunctions into two types: CO-ORDINATING and SUBORDINATING. The difference between them is that a co-ordinating conjunction unites two sentence units of equal rank, whereas a subordinating conjunction unites a subordinate clause to a clause of higher rank. Conjunctions normally come at the beginning of their clauses, and subordinating conjunctions are attached to the front of the subordinate clause. In this respect conjunctions differ from adverbs, particularly conjuncts which have a similar linking function, since the latter need not appear at the head of their own clause. Some conjuncts, such as *however*, are more commonly found as the second or third word of a clause. A clause introduced by a subordinating conjunction cannot normally stand alone as a complete sentence, though particularly in spoken language this may happen through ellipsis where the context allows the rest of the sentence to be understood. The difference between subordination and co-ordination may not be large, and it may be more a feature of emphasis and background than of anything else. Common co-ordinating conjunctions are *and* and *but*, and subordinating ones *when* and *because*. In *When the boat was hit by a torpedo, it sank*, the clause introduced by *when* is subordinate because it could not form a complete sentence in itself. This clause is subordinate to *it sank*, which could form a sentence on its own. The sinking is made more important than the fact that the boat was hit by a torpedo, which is introduced as an explanation of why it sunk. The sinking is put in the foreground and the fact that the ship was hit by a torpedo is part of the background. It would, however, be quite possible to rephrase that sentence as *The boat was hit by a torpedo and it sank*. Here both clauses are of equal rank, for each could stand as a separate sentence. Both clauses are foregrounded. There remains a causal connection between the two since it is understood that it was because it was hit by a torpedo that the boat sank; but that causal link is not expressed. Formally both clauses are of equal weight, though some readers might well think one was nevertheless more important than the other. At all events these examples show that there may not be a great gap between subordination and co-ordination.

Co-ordinating conjunctions link together two units of language which are of equal rank, whether they are clauses or not. Two subordinate clauses may be united by a co-ordinating conjunction, as in *After the ship hit the mine and caught fire, it sank*. Here both *after* and *the ship* refer to *hit the mine* and *caught fire*. This example shows that with co-ordinating conjunctions some ellipsis is allowed, since *the ship* or a pronoun equivalent is not necessary before *caught*. This is not possible with subordinating conjunctions. We cannot say *After the ship was hit by a torpedo, sank*, although we can have *The ship was hit by a torpedo and sank*. Co-ordinating conjunctions join together individual words, phrases, groups or clauses; for example, two nouns can be linked by *and* as in *bread and butter*. When several items are linked together, it is customary to join only the last two with *and*, as in *The Navy, Army and Air Force recruit students direct from university*. It is not necessary to introduce an *and* between *Navy* and *Army*. If multiple units are joined together with varying conjunctions, it may lead to ambiguity as to what precisely is being linked. In the example *Shall we ask Helen and Jane or Bill?* it is possible to think that Bill is an alternative to Jane or to both Helen and Jane.

Subordinate clauses can come before or after the clause to which they refer, and the subordinating conjunction will come at its head. As co-ordinating conjunctions join together two units of equal rank, the co-ordinating conjunction will come between the two items; it cannot come at the head of the first item. The sentence *When he drank too much, he always had a headache* can also be formulated as *He always had a headache when he drank too much.* But this is not true with co-ordination. *He went home and she was very angry* cannot be rephrased as *And she was very angry, he went home.* However, some co-ordination is expressed through two co-ordinating conjunctions rather than through one; these conjunctions are known as CORRELATIVES. Examples of this are *either . . . or* and *both . . . and.* In such cases there will be a conjunction at the head of each unit which is linked: *Either he goes or I do.* It is characteristic of traditional grammar that correlatives should unite only two units (and no more) and that the units should be of the same syntactic rank and structure, although this type of restriction is readily flouted in informal language. It is claimed that *either* and *both* can refer only to two things, and so a sentence such as *We can go to either Paris or Nice or Cannes for our holidays* would by many be considered ungrammatical. This is because *either* originally meant 'one of two things', and to some extent this meaning still survives. If someone said *You can do either*, we would assume only two alternatives were available. In most cases it is just as easy to avoid *either* altogether, for the sentence above could be expressed as *We can go to Paris, Nice or Cannes for our holidays.* Since this second formulation is shorter and just as intelligible, it may seem preferable to use it. The situation is rather different with respect to the joining of two unequal units. This can be illustrated by *He likes to get up early and a cooked breakfast*, which could be understood to mean *He likes to get up early and he likes a cooked breakfast.* But the syntactic organisation of each predicate is different and hence it is felt by many unacceptable to link them directly by *and* as is done above. How acceptable such sentences are depends to some extent on the disparity in the syntactic organisation of the units being joined.

As we have seen already in this chapter, interjections are not unlike disjuncts. They add some emotional overtone to the sentence in which they occur, though they stand outside the formal structure of that sentence. Interjections are part of the discourse strategy which we adopt in order to make sure the listener or, though less often, the reader is paying attention and understands the tone intended. Many of them consist of sequences of sounds which are unusual in English or which would not normally be considered full words. If a mother says to her child *Sh! go to sleep*, we would have to understand *Sh* as an interjection, though it would not otherwise be recognised as a complete word. Many interjections have a traditional representation in writing, which may give them a spurious word quality. That clicking sound which indicates regret or disapproval may in writing be represented as *tut*, which is a form having all the characteristics of a word though it is not a very good representation of the actual sound made. For the most part interjections are not likely to cause difficulty in analysis.

5 Recapitulation and Development

It was pointed out in the Introduction that traditional grammar is a word-based grammar and in principle it works from words to larger units of language. It will have become apparent in the intervening chapters that it is difficult to limit one's attention in analysing English to words alone in so far as words in English have few inflexional endings. For this reason what grammatical category a word belongs to may only become clear through a consideration of the function a word has in the sentence as a whole; the form of the word will not be sufficient in itself to reveal its class. The same word can function as noun, verb or adjective, and it is only when it is used in a sentence that one can decide to what category it belongs in that instance. There is no match in English between the ending or form of words and grammatical categories. Hence any study of grammar must also introduce elements of sentence function. However, even function is not without its problems, for those who are not used to analysing sentences in English will be immediately struck by the circular nature of some of the definitions: a subject will be defined in relation to the verb, and a verb in relation to the subject. To know one you need to know the other, and this is clearly a problem when you start undertaking analysis. Thus a common definition of a subject is that it is that part of the sentence which undertakes the action of the verb; and equally a verb may be defined as the action which the subject performs. This type of circular definition is probably inevitable in discussions of function, as the various parts of a sentence are interrelated and can only be understood functionally in the way in which they affect one another. Since part of the way in which one can characterise a noun is that it can act as the subject of a sentence, the circularity of functional definition may affect our ability to decide what is or what is not a noun.

Another help in determining what is the subject of a sentence is the word order, which in English is fairly rigid. In statements, unlike commands and questions, the subject always precedes the verb. This applies only to standard written prose, since poets often make use of a different word order in order to create ambiguity. The subject always precedes the verb in a declarative sentence, and as a general rule these will be the first and second items in a clause, although it is possible to introduce an adverb either as the first element or as the second element between the subject and the verb. In any English sentence one would expect such a pattern as *The students were late*, in which the subject is *the students* (which is a noun group) and the verb is *were* (which is a verb group). An adverb such as *usually* can be inserted at the beginning or in the middle of the sentence, and, if a sentence were made up to illustrate the first instance, the subject would be the second rather than the first item in it, as in *Usually the students were late*. What is important is to recognise that there are various ways in which one can decide what category a word belongs to, and with a little practice this type of analysis should prove relatively straightforward. I shall, however, be dealing with the make-up of sentences in more detail in the chapters which follow.

Traditional grammar is word-based, but it has to be accepted that it may on occasion be difficult to decide precisely what is a word. Conventions change, particularly with respect to spelling and hyphens. Some people prefer to write *a fifteenth century church* as *a fifteenth-century church*, and so would have to accept that in this latter case *fifteenth-century* was a single word which was an adjective. In some cases what had been two words in the past may come to be spelt with a hyphen or even as a single word without a hyphen. It is possible now to find *fifteenthcentury* as an adjective written as a single word, though that is still quite rare. We also saw in discussing prepositions that some of them are complex and consist of two or three words, such as *because of* and *in front of*. Although these are multi-word prepositions, they have to be treated as single words. The same applies to conjunctions, although here some examples may be written as single words, especially in American English. Thus *in so far as* may be seen written as *insofaras*. Multi-word conjunctions were rather more frequent in earlier varieties of English than they are today. In Elizabethan English is was quite possible to add *that* to conjunctions such as *if* and *when* to form complex forms such as *if that* and *when that*.

When one starts to analyse English sentences, it is important to remember the linear nature of language. When you look at the sentences in this book, you can see that everything proceeds in a line: one letter follows another to make a word, one word follows another to make a sentence. The same applies to speech, which is a sequence of individual sounds. You have to read words in the order in which they occur, just as you have to listen to sounds in the sequence in which they are uttered. You cannot read or listen to a whole number of words at the same time. There is a recognised system for reading English, by which we begin at the top left-hand corner of a page and work across the top line of writing from left to right. When we get to the end of one line, we proceed to the left-hand edge of the line below and read from left to right and so on till the end of the page. This is very different from the way in which we 'read' a picture. Think of the many portraits of the Queen there are. We can, when we look at one, assimilate the whole portrait at once; we do not start in the top left-hand corner and gradually work our way down to the bottom right-hand. We can naturally focus on a particular part of the portrait, if we wish, but there will be no set way in which this will be done. Some might focus first on the background, and others on the disposition of the hands. But the portrait will be thought of as a whole which cannot readily be broken down into its constituent parts. How different this is from language. A description of somebody would have to proceed in some order; even a description of a portrait would have to decide what feature it would comment on first. It would be impossible to see a written description as a whole in the same way as a portrait. The items would be presented in a sequence, and each sentence would be arranged as a series of individual words which would have to be read in the order in which they occur.

Each feature of language can be combined with other similar features to make up a more important unit of language, just as various letters can be combined to make up a word and various words to make up a sentence. In other words, language works in a hierarchical way, in which each unit can be combined with others to make a higher unit, and that in turn can be combined with others like it to make yet a higher unit. This is something which has already been implied in earlier chapters in so far as we have referred to nouns and noun groups. A noun group consists of one or more words to fulfil the same function as a noun. Language consists of a series of segments, and each segment can be united with other segments to form larger units. It is important to understand what these segments are, and equally how one should read them. In a linear arrangement one has to understand how the parts are grouped to form larger segments, or else faulty communication can occur. This may be illustrated by the rules applied to mathematical symbols. Although in mathematics brackets mean multiplication, they have to be resolved in a different order from the actual multiplication sign. Thus $2 (5 + 4)$ would give a different answer from $2 \times 5 + 4$. Since what is inside the brackets has to be tackled first, $2 (5 + 4)$ means 2×9, which gives 18. But in $2 \times 5 + 4$, the multiplication has to be done first so we have $10 + 4$, which gives 14. Unless you understand the sequence in which the various symbols have to be read and follow the instructions in the correct order, you could easily come to the wrong conclusion. In the examples given above, the same numbers can produce different answers because the order in which the steps have to be undertaken are not the same. The same is true of words, for the way in which they are taken together affects the meaning of the sentence as a whole. For example, it is not uncommon at the moment among teenagers to use *brilliant* as a word of commendation, in which emotional approval is the strongest element in the word's meaning. Hence to a teenager *a brilliant white paint* might well mean a white paint which evoked a high degree of approval. To older people *a brilliant white paint* is more likely to mean a paint which is brilliant white in colour. The difference lies in whether *brilliant* is understood as an intensifier of *white* or as a modifier of *paint*. In speech this may be made clear through intonation; in writing one has to rely on punctuation of one sort or another to help the reader. In the example where *brilliant* is an intensifier to *white*, some people might prefer to hyphenate the words as *brilliant-white* in order to prevent ambiguity.

If we start with words and go up the hierarchical order, we can arrange the different parts of a sentence on the following scale: words – (phrases) – groups – clauses – sentences. I have arranged them in an ascending order, in which it could be said that each step on the scale is made up of one or more units on the immediately preceding step. Thus a sentence consists of one or more clauses; a clause consists of one or more groups; a group consists of one or more phrases; and a phrase consists of one or more words. I have put the unit 'phrase' in brackets, because it is not an essential step in the progression from word to sentence; all the other steps will be found in every sentence. Thus *man* is a word, which with other words can form a group as in *the happy man*, which is a noun group. This noun group will be linked with other groups to form a clause, as in *The happy man lived in Sheffield*, which consists of a noun group (*The happy man*), a verb group (*lived*) and an adverb group (*in Sheffield*). This clause can be linked with other clauses to form a sentence, as in *The happy man lived in Sheffield, but he worked in Manchester every day*, in which there are two clauses. It may be seen that it is possible to make up one step in the hierarchy by using only one of the immediately lower items on the hierarchical scale. *The happy man lived in Sheffield* may be said to be a clause, but that could form a sentence on its own. The verb *lived* is a single word, but it forms a whole group, a verb group; and so a group may consist of one word, even if it more often consists of several. Equally the noun group *the happy man*, which has three words, could have been represented by the single pronoun *he*, which is only one word. Although it is unusual for a single word to act as a clause on its own, it is possible with commands such as *Jump*. This is a single word, which forms a verb group, and this verb group in its turn forms a clause which is a complete sentence.

It may be time now to provide some definitions of these units of language, though it must be stressed how difficult it is to provide watertight definitions. In many cases it is necessary to refer to the other elements of language to provide definitions. The concept of word was discussed in the Introduction, and nothing further needs to be added here. A GROUP consists of one or more words which together constitute a functional unit, such as subject, of a clause. This means that a group will always be acting as subject, verb (which I shall from now on refer to as predicator when it is a clause element), complement, object or adjunct of a clause. In this way one can distinguish between a word which is part of a group and one which forms a group on its own. In *Man is a rational animal, man* is both a word and a group, since by itself it forms the subject of the clause; but in *The man in the blue suit is a Russian, man* is a word within the noun group *The man in the blue suit* and naturally *man* does not in this case constitute a group on its own. The PHRASE occupies a medial position between the word and the group. It differs from a word in that it consists of more than one word. It differs from a group in that a group will always form a functional unit such as a subject, whereas a phrase only forms part of a group. The last example cited, *The man in the blue suit*, is a noun group consisting of determiner, head and qualifier. The qualifier is a prepositional phrase, which has the preposition *with* and its completive *the blue suit*. This prepositional phrase clearly does not form a group by itself. It is possible to have prepositional phrases which function as groups. The phrase *in the blue suit* can itself function as an adjunct in a clause, as for example in the sentence *Today he turned up in the blue suit*. But in this case one would say that *in the blue suit* was an adverb group which was made up of a prepositional phrase, in the same way as *late* could be an adverb group which was made up of a word. The phrase which occurs most frequently is the prepositional phrase, but there is also the adjective phrase. A CLAUSE consists of one or more groups, at least one of which normally functions as subject and the other as predicator.

In speaking and reading English we refer, if only subconsciously, to the order of the words and the hierarchy of the linguistic units. The words must occur in a particular order to constitute a group, and the groups will be positioned in a particular order so that the function each one has in the clause will be readily understood. A certain amount of flexibility is allowed, but this is not very large. As we saw earlier, a noun group is put together of determiner, modifier, head and qualifier, though only the head is an essential part of the noun group. It is through the organisation of the noun group that we can tell which word is acting as head in so far as single words act as modifiers and precede the head, whereas phrases act as qualifiers and follow the head. The head will therefore be the last single free-standing word. In *The Labour Party proposal for a different tax system was defeated*, we recognise that *The Labour Party proposal for a different tax system* is the subject and hence forms a noun group. In the noun group *proposal* is the final free-standing single word, since *for a different tax system* hangs together as a prepositional phrase and so must be the qualifier. The head of this group is *proposal*. Both *Labour* and *Party* are often nouns in English and could in other noun groups act as their head, but in this particular noun group since they are followed by the single free-standing word *proposal* they must be acting as modifiers. Some flexibility is possible in that single words do occasionally follow the head of a noun group. In *The conclusion above is untenable* the subject is *The conclusion above* and here the head *conclusion* is followed by the single word *above*. But this flouting of the normal structure of the group is unusual in standard prose because it would make comprehension difficult if it occurred too often.

In the previous chapters three groups have been introduced: the noun, verb and adverb groups. There is one other group, the adjective group, which needs to be characterised, though it may be said that it occurs far less frequently than the others. As its name implies, an adjective group fulfils the same function as an adjective, though only in those cases where an adjective stands by itself and fulfils some independent function within a clause. In *The happy man*, *happy* is an adjective which has no independent function within a clause since it is acting as a modifier within a noun group. But if that phrase were to be rewritten as *The man is happy*, then *happy* is no longer a modifier within a noun group for it is functioning by itself as a complement of the verb *to be*. In view of this function as complement, it is consistent to think that *happy* is a group, which can be defined as an adjective group. This group can be expanded in ways that are not possible for an adjective which is acting as a modifier of a noun group. Thus the sentence could read *The man is happy in his work*, in which *in his work* is a prepositional phrase which is acting as a qualifer of *happy*. It is not possible to add this kind of prepositional phrase to a modifier in a noun group; we cannot say *The happy in his work man* because modifiers in noun groups are single words. An adjective group is commonly met with only as the complement of verbs such as *to be* or of those which take an object and a complement, which will be treated more fully in a later chapter. It is possible to have such a sentence as *The increase in salary made him happy in his work*, in which *him* is the object and *happy in his work* the complement. An adjective group has a composition which resembles that of the noun group: it consists of a head, which will normally be an adjective. That head can be followed by a qualifier, which consists of a phrase as in the example quoted above, and it can be preceded by a modifier which acts as an intensifier of the adjective head. Hence in the sentence *He is very happy in his work* there is an adjective group *very happy in his work*. This consists of the intensifier *very*, the head *happy*, and the qualifier *in his work*. Although noun groups are usually fairly elaborate, this is less usual with adjective groups, which more often than not consist of a single word.

We have so far referred to the various steps in the hierarchy of the sentence as though these were entirely independent segments which were related to one another simply by the order they have in the sentence and hence by the function which they carry out. To a large extent this is true, because English words do not change their form very much, and some of the changes which they can undergo are ones of meaning rather than of grammatical function. Most count nouns have a distinctive form for the singular and another for the plural, and this is usually indicated through the absence or presence of a final -*(e)s*. Although this change is essentially one of meaning, for the final -*(e)s* indicates more than one, it can also have repercussions on the form of other words in the same sentence if the word in the plural is the subject of the sentence. A subject in the plural will be followed by a verb in the base form if it is in the present tense; but a subject in the singular will be followed by a verb in the -*s* form if it is in the present tense. Hence we find *They love Sheffield*, with *love* in the base form, but *He loves Sheffield*, with *loves* in the -*s* form because it is following a subject which is singular. The principle that the form of one grammatical unit in a sentence is influenced by the features of a different unit within the same sentence is referred to as CONCORD. In English, which has few endings, it is principally found in the relationship between a subject and the verb in the present tense.

The normal rule for subject–verb concord is that a singular subject requires the verb of the present tense in the -*s* form when the subject is a third person one. This is no variation in person in the verb forms of the preterite, and some verbs, such as the modal auxiliaries, have no -*s* form in the present tense. The verb *to be* has a first person singular ending in the present tense (*am*) as well as a first and third person singular form of the preterite (*was*) which differs from the other persons of the preterite (*were*). This means that with the verb *to be* a first person subject, which essentially means *I*, will be followed by the form *am* in the present and *was* in the preterite. Although the rule for subject–verb concord is apparently simple, it can lead to problems simply because it is not always certain whether the subject is singular or not; different speakers may take certain words and phrases, particular collective nouns, as either singular or plural. A collective noun refers to a gathering of people or animals which can be considered as singular because they are acting together or as a plural because the group consists of a number of. individuals who are thought of as separate. Thus *government* may be thought of as a single entity which represents a faceless authority and so it may be treated as singular; or it may be considered as a group of people who should not be considered as losing their separate identities even though they are acting together. In some cases it may be possible to introduce shades of meaning according to whether one treats a collective noun as singular or plural. If one says *The government is stupid*, one means that the laws and other actions of the government are foolish without implying that its individual members are; but if one were to say that *The government are stupid*, one might well wish to imply that the individuals who make up the government are all to be considered foolish. While it is possible to read such a distinction into the use of *is* or *are*, most people probably do not exploit it in their usage.

There are many other cases where variation exists in subject–verb concord. Usually when a subject consists of two co-ordinate heads (that is, when the subject is a noun group with two heads joined together by *and*), the verb goes into the plural or base form: *Tim and John are here*. But, if the subject is thought to form a single notional entity such as *bread and butter* or *fish and chips*, then a singular verb with the *-s* form may be used. When two modifiers in a noun group are linked by *and*, which may imply that each refers to a separate item, then the verb may take the plural form. Thus a noun group such as *English and American football* may be taken to imply two types of football, one English and the other American, and this could result in a plural verb: *English and American football are dangerous*. The plural sense is much clearer if *both* is included before *English*. In this type of example it must be admitted that variation between singular and plural is not uncommon, particularly in those cases where *both* is not included. More controversial for prescriptive grammarians has been the presence of *or* within a nominal group. With a subject such as *John or Tim*, the grammarian's normal reaction is to understand this to mean *either* John *or* Tim and to recommend that a singular verb should follow, so that in *John or Tim is there* the sense would be something like *Either John is there or Tim is there*. But in speech at least it is more usual to hear *John of Tim are there*. There are many other instances where *and* or *or* create problems of concord similar to these outlined above. Spoken language is much more flexible in its attitude to concord and is more likely to be influenced by the idea behind the expression than precise grammatical concord. In written language strict concord is more commonly insisted on, but even there some expressions seem so unnatural to most speakers of the language that they now tend to be avoided. This applies particularly to concord with the verb *to be*, which has the complication of the first person singular form *am* as well as the third person singular *is*. Hence in a sentence such as *Neither he nor I am going*, grammarians have tended to insist on *am* because the verb agrees with the nearest element of a co-ordinate subject. So *He is not going* and *I am not going* should be combined to form *Neither he nor I am going*. But this sentence feels awkward to most speakers of the language, and colloquially it would almost certainly appear as *Neither he nor I are going*. In writing the awkwardness is best avoided by rewriting.

The verb *to be* is also involved in other types of concord in so far as it is a relational verb which has a complement which is in direct relation with the subject. To say *That man is a professor* implies that *man* and *professor* refer to the same human being: the complement is the same person as the subject. With personal pronouns which distinguish subject and complement forms – for example, *I* is the first person subject form and *me* its non-subject or complement form – it has been a shibboleth of traditional grammarians that the verb *to be* should be followed by the pronoun in the subject form. Hence it was in the past frequently recommended that one should say *It's I* rather than *It's me*. This has not been insisted upon for other persons so strongly, and *It's them* (rather than *It's they*) does not arouse the passions of older people to the same extent as *It's me*. It may now be said that the insistence on *It's I* has disappeared, and it is accepted that the non-subject pronoun can follow the verb *to be*. However, the verb *to be* can still cause problems to speakers of the language, because there may not be a strict agreement in number between the subject and the complement. For example, in *It's those students next door again* the subject *it* is singular whereas the complement *those students* is plural. In this case we all accept that the verb has to be in the singular to agree with *it*. But there are many instances where the verb may be attracted to the complement, and this is particularly so where the subject and complement can easily change roles. With *It's those students next door again* one cannot rearrange subject and complement to give *Those students next door are it again.* But *The two youngest children are my biggest headache* could easily be rearranged as *My biggest headache is the two youngest children.* In the latter example it would be not uncommon to use *are* instead of *is* in speech.

Concord has also caused difficulty in the relationship between personal pronouns and indefinite and interrogative pronouns. It is generally accepted that indefinite pronouns such as *everyone* and interrogative pronouns such as *who?* are singular in so far as the verb dependent upon these forms as subject goes into the third person singular. We say *Is everyone happy?* and not *Are everyone happy?*, just as we say *Who is coming to tea?* rather than *Who are coming to tea?*, even though more than one person may be involved in each case. The problem occurs when you also have a personal pronoun or possessive adjective which refers back to the indefinite or interrogative pronoun. Traditionally the form used would have been *he* or *his*, since the masculine gender has been used in English to imply both male and female. But the use of the singular was often felt by speakers of the language to be unsatisfactory since the real reference was to more than one person. More recently this usage has come under attack from feminist writers as well, who feel that the use of the masculine form to imply females as well is unacceptable. The attack by feminists has merely reinforced a tendency already apparent in the languge which was to use a plural. The plural form is understood to refer to individuals as a group and it has the advantage in English that it is not gender-specific. So now one could say that it is accepted that a plural personal pronoun or possessive adjective may be employed even when the verb is in the singular. A sentence such as *Is everyone sitting at their proper desks?* would now be generally acceptable, though it may cause discomfort to some purists. It may be seen, however, that there is a further problem of concord in that sentence. When the possessive was in the singular then the noun which was part of the same group would also be in the singular to give *Is everyone sitting at his proper desk?* Because of the feeling that each person has only one desk to sit at, it is possible to let the noun remain in the singular even though the preceding possessive adjective is plural, to give *Is everyone sitting at their proper desk?* It may be gathered from this that concord is in somewhat a fluid state at the moment because of the conflicting pressures to which it has been subjected – notional concord, grammatical concord and feminism.

In our discussions so far there is one aspect of language which has not been touched on and that is negation. Words which indicate negation fall into different word classes. The principal negator is *not*, which is an adverb; but *no* may be either an adverb or an adjective. It acts as an adjective in such sentences as *There's no sense in going on.* In this position it can be regarded as a determiner in a noun group, because it cannot be used in association with other determiners such as *the* or *my*. In the form *none* it is a predicative adjective or the head of an adjective group. There are of course other ways of providing a negative sense, though not all these other methods involve words. Some may consist of prefixes such as *dis-*, *non-* and *un-* in such words as *disloyal, non-combatant* and *unlikely*. Because words of negation may be either adverbs or adjectives, the way a sentence may be turned into its negative equivalent varies. An adverb such as *not* will be attached to the verb group, whereas an adjective such as *no* will be part of a noun group. The use of a negator in a noun group may well mean that the scope of the negation is rather more localised and restricted than when a negator is attached to the verb group. This means that when a negator is part of the verb group we usually understand the whole clause as negated, but when it is attached to a noun group it may be only that group in the whole clause which is negated. This is particularly true when *not* acts as an adverb which is an intensifier within a noun, or for that matter an adverb, group. There is essentially no difference in negation between *We didn't get a report this year* and *We got no report this year*, for the negation extends to the whole sentence. But in a sentence such as *We got a not very promising report*, the meaning of the negation is restricted to the noun clause. In the first two examples no report was received; but in the third a report was received, but this was negative in its contents. The same would apply to a negator attached to an adverb which was a disjunct: *Not surprisingly, he arrived two hours late.* In such instances the use of *not* is less common than that of a negative prefix. The use of *not* within a noun group is more frequent when there is another negative element in the noun group as well, as in *It was a not unexpected result.* Here the two negatives cancel each other out to suggest that the result was expected, even if the sense of expectation is not as strong as it would be if one had said *It was the expected result.*

In the verb group *not* is added to create negation in standard English, though in other varieties words such as *never* may also be employed: *you never did* correspond to *you didn't.* If the verb group has a part of the verb *to be* or *to have* as its head, then the negator is simply included in the group. With all other verbs it is necessary to include an auxiliary, and the negator is normally included between the auxiliary and the head. Hence we have forms such as *He did not arrive on time*; *He has not arrived yet*; *He will not arrive before seven.* If there is no auxiliary in the verb group in its positive form, then the auxiliary that has to be included in the negative form is *do.* The *not* adverb is regularly contracted to *n't* in the spoken language, and increasingly in the written language too. With auxiliaries that are contracted in positive clauses, there are two possible forms when a negative is included: one with the auxiliary contracted and the other with the negator contracted. The negative of *He's here* is either *He's not here* or *He isn't here.*

Although it might at first sight seem easy enough to decide when a sentence is negative, this is not quite the case. In addition to words such as *not* and *never*, there are other words which operate syntactically as negators though they might not seem to be negative words. This applies for example to words such as *seldom* or *hardly.* The reason for saying this is that negative clauses have certain characteristics which come under the general heading of concord, which we have been dealing with in this chapter. When a verb group is negated, then what are called assertive forms (such as *somebody* and *already*) have to be turned into non-assertive forms (such as *anybody* and *yet*). Hence the positive sentences *He's there already* and *There's someone there* have the negative forms *He isn't there yet* and *There isn't anyone there.* In addition negative sentences affect the tag questions, such as *Is he?* and *Isn't he?*, which can be added at the end of sentences in English. Positive sentences are followed by negative tag questions, and negative sentences are followed by positive tags. Hence *He's there already, isn't he?* has as its negative counterpart *He's not there yet, is he?*, in which the positive *He's there* has the negative tag *isn't he?*, and the negative *He's not there* has the positive tag *is he?*. Bearing these syntactic features in mind we can see that there are a number of words which are understood by the speakers of the language to have a negative input even though they appear not to be negative in form. These words include adverbs such as *hardly* as well as adjectives such as *little*. The non-assertive equivalent of *some* is *any*, which is the form you find after *little* in such sentences as *There was little material assistance I could offer to any of them*. The sense of *little* here is to be understood as negative, meaning essentially 'none at all'. The same applies to adverbs such as *hardly*, as in the sentence *Dorinda hardly ever does any practice*. In addition to these words which always take non-assertive forms and positive tags, there are others, particularly verbs and adjectives, which may be followed by non-assertive forms and by negative tags. These words imply negation, though the immediate sense may seem positive. For example, the verb *deny* appears to be positive, but clearly implies that something that has been stated is *not* true. Hence the negative sense demands a non-assertive form such as *any* rather than *some*, but the positive form of the verb equally demands a negative tag, as in *You denied that you said anything, didn't you?*

Traditionally in English the negator has often been weakened in pronunciation, as is true with the contraction of *not* to *n't*, and this has led to the need to provide some further emphasis when the negative sense has to be strengthened. In speech this can be done through stress, but both there and in writing it is more characteristic to add some form of intensification. This intensification may be done through intensifiers which precede the negator, as in *Absolutely no admittance*, but it is more usually achieved through the addition of some intensifying prepositional phrase which is added either immediately after the negator or at the end of the clause. The latter is the more usual position with the negator *not*. Although it is possible to have either *There's nothing at all wrong with him* or *There's nothing wrong with him at all*, one cannot rephrase *I don't like him in the least* as *I do not in the least like him*.

6   The Make-up of Clauses

Traditional grammar is a word-based grammar, and so in this book hitherto I have used words as the basic linguistic building-blocks and seen how they can be combined to form larger units in language. These larger units consist of either phrases or groups. Groups are usually characterised by the role they play in the clause, and so it may be appropriate now to leave the word-based methodology to focus on the clause and its constituent parts. To do this it is easier to work from the clause and then to analyse its make-up. In other words we shall in this chapter not work up from small units to larger ones, but we shall work down from a larger linguistic unit, the clause, to those parts of which it is composed. This approach has also been employed as a subsidiary methodology in traditional grammar, which has investigated such features as subject and predicate, but it is even more common in modern grammars which have tended to start from the sentence in their grammatical methodology. Unfortunately it is even more difficult to provide a satisfactory definition of a clause than it is to provide one for a word. For the moment it may suffice to say that as a rule each clause contains one finite verb.

In traditional grammar it was customary to say that a sentence consisted of a subject and predicate. The subject is the same in traditional as in modern grammar. The predicate is the rest of a sentence. This terminology was developed because many sentences consist only of a subject and its verb, such as *He came*. It therefore appeared as though subject and predicate were the two essential parts of a sentence, so that if one had a sentence such as *He sent the parcel by air freight* it would still consist only of these two elements. In this latter example *he* is the subject, but the predicate is *sent the parcel by air freight*. In some ways there is something to be said for this simple division between subject and predicate. It also has several disadvantages. The predicates will in most cases have to be broken down further by analysis and it will then become apparent that there is not much unity in the various predicates that are possible. Furthermore, the concept of predicate suggests that all the elements in it are of the same importance in the sentence, though it is possible to re-order the elements so that individual ones receive greater emphasis. Thus *He arrived suddenly* might be rephrased as *Suddenly he arrived*. In both instances the predicate would consist of *arrived suddenly*, but the two predicates are very different in weight, tone and emphasis. There does not seem sufficient reason to have a division into subject and predicate alone. A slightly more detailed division is much more informative about the structure of English.

At present, therefore, a common division of the sentence is into the following units: subject, predicator (and notice that this is not the same thing as the predicate), object, complement and adjunct. Although these units can exist in different forms, they form the only five possible units of any clause. This means that all clauses are formed from permutations of these units and that the expansion of clauses must take place through the development or multiple occurrence of these units. It is time now to explain the meaning of these terms and to relate them to the world classes which have been discussed previously.

The SUBJECT is the word or words performing the action indicated by the predicator, but it may also be thought of as the word or words constituting the topic or concept which the rest of the clause elaborates upon. In *The boy loves the girl*, it is *the boy* who is doing the action of the verb *loves* and is the subject. Similarly *the boy* is the topic which the rest of the clause expands, since the rest of the sentence tells us something about this boy. Although it is unlikely that most speakers of English will have any difficulty in deciding what is the subject of a clause, there are some instances where the subject may not seem to fit the definitions given above. This applies particularly to those sentences in which *it* is the subject, because it may be used as what is called a dummy or empty subject. In the example *it's a pity that they couldn't come to tea*, the subject is *it*. But that *it* stands in place of the real topic of the sentence, which is *they couldn't come to tea*. It is the fact that the people could not come to tea which is the reason for the expression of sorrow. *It*, therefore, acts as a dummy subject for the real topic of the sentence, which is *that they couldn't come to tea*; but from a grammatical point of view *it* is the subject of the verb *is*. In addition to the definitions of subject given earlier which involve meaning, it may also be said that in English clauses the subject comes before the predicator in statements and it commonly occurs as the first word of a clause.

In an earlier chapter on the noun and related words it was stated that a noun group could be identified as a group of words which could act as the subject of a clause. This definition may now have to be modified. It might well be asked why, if a noun group is the subject of a clause, there is any need to have two technical terms, noun group and subject. In fact, as we saw earlier, a noun group can occur in other positions in a clause and so a noun group does not always act as the subject of a clause. It may, for example, act as an adverb group. Equally it is not true to say that all subjects are noun groups, though the majority of them are. It is possible to have one clause as the subject of another one. Consider the sentence *'I hate you' is not a very nice thing to say to the postman*. Here the verb *is* has as its subject *I hate you*, which I have put in inverted commas in the example; that is what is not a nice thing and so forms the topic which the rest of the sentence expands. But *I hate you* is itself a clause containing a subject *I* and a verb *hate*. The mechanism whereby one clause can be incorporated in another clause is something which will need comment later. For our purposes at the moment it is important to realise that, although subjects are usually noun groups, they may also be clauses.

The PREDICATOR is less difficult to characterise, since it always consists of a verb group. The predicator is the verb (or verb group) which embodies the action or indicates the state of the subject. In the earlier example *The boy loves the girl*, we saw that *the boy* was the subject. The predicator is *loves*, for that is the action which the boy is performing. But the predicator can be a stative verb which indicates a state rather than embodies an action. In a sentence such as *The boy is stupid*, the subject is still *the boy*. The predicator is in this instance *is*, for that indicates the state of the subject. In negative sentences, the negator is closely linked with the verb group, but is not part of it as it belongs to the adverb word class. Although the subject may be represented by a clause rather than by a noun group, this is not true of the predicator for its function may never be occupied by a clause. It is only a verb group which can fill this role. As a general rule in declarative sentences, the predicator follows the subject directly and so is usually the second element in a clause. In speech the verb group may be contracted so that only the auxiliary, whether modal or non-modal, is included. To the question *Are you coming tomorrow?*, the answer might be *No, I'm not*. In this answer the *'m* (for *am*) stands for *am coming*; but it still represents the verb group or predicator in this sentence.

The OBJECT and the COMPLEMENT have many points of similarity. They both come after the predicator and each normally consists of a noun group, though there are variations as we shall see. They differ in that the object never refers back to the subject, whereas the complement usually does. If we consider the two sentences *He is king* and *He killed the king*, in the first *king* is the same person as *he* and so it acts as a complement, but in the second *the king* is not the same person as *he* and so it acts as an object. In the chapter on verb groups we saw that verbs were of various types. They can be transitive or intransitive, and they can be stative or dynamic. These differences are fundamental in distinguishing objects and complements. Verbs which are intransitive take neither object nor complement. This is particularly true of verbs of motion. A verb such as *arrive* will take no object or complement. *He arrived*, which consists of subject and predicator, is a complete sentence. If a verb such as *arrive* is followed by anything, it will be followed by an adjunct, as in *He arrived yesterday*. Here the *yesterday* answers the question When?, which is a marker of an adverb, the word class which normally occupies the adjunct function. Transitive verbs are those verbs which take a direct object, as in *He killed the king*. The object can usually be identified by making it the subject of a passive sentence: *The king was killed by him*. Here *the king*, which was the direct object in the previous example, has been turned into the subject. Dynamic verbs can be either transitive or intransitive. Stative verbs, as the name suggests, indicate a state and hence are likely to be followed by a complement, for that state will include both subject and complement. The verb *to be* in the sentence *He is king* indicates a state rather than an action. It is dynamic verbs which embody an action. Stative verbs may be followed by an adjective group as well as by a noun group. It is possible to have *He is happy* as well as *He is king*; in the first the complement is an adjective group *happy*, and in the second a noun group *king*. Both, of course, refer back to the subject *he*. Objects cannot be formed by an adjective group, because objects do not refer back to the subject. Hence an object must contain a noun or pronoun to introduce the concept or thing referred to which is different from the subject. A complement can consist of an adjective group precisely because it can refer back to the subject, and hence the concept or thing which is being referred to is already given. An adjective group must have something to which it refers, as is true of any adjective.

Objects are divided into two categories: DIRECT and INDIRECT. The direct object is easier to characterise, and traditionally it has been defined as that part of the clause which suffers the action of the verb. The subject initiates and carries out the action, and the direct object suffers the action. In *He killed the king, he* is the subject because he undertakes the action of killing and *the king* is the direct object because the king suffers the action of killing. The subject is the who or what that carries out the action, and the direct object is the who or what that suffers the action. The direct object is normally represented by a noun group, but it can, like the subject, be represented by a clause. In the sentence *Dorinda said she was bored*, the subject is *Dorinda* and the predicator *said*. The direct object is *she was bored*, because it is what was said; to that extent it may be claimed to suffer the action of the verb, in this case *said*.

Some verbs can have two objects, and when that happens the first of the two objects will be the indirect object and the second the direct object. In the sentence *She gave the postman a glass of water*, the subject is *she* and the predicator *gave*. There are two objects, the first of which is *the postman* and the second *a glass of water*. The first is an indirect object. What is given is the glass of water, and hence the name DIRECT OBJECT. The INDIRECT OBJECT is so called because it indicates to whom the action of the verb is directed. As is true in this case, the indirect object is nearly always an animate and it may be recognised because it can be replaced by a prepositional phrase or left out altogether. Our example could be rewritten as *She gave a glass of water to the postman* or even as *She gave a glass of water*. When the indirect object is not expressed as a prepositional phrase, it always precedes the direct object, and that means it comes directly after the predicator. The direct object may never be omitted in those clauses in which it occurs because transitive verbs demand an object. Hence it would not be possible to have such a sentence as *She gave to the postman*, for this sentence is incomplete in that the transitive verb *to give* has no object, which is obligatory for it. However, there are a few isolated verbs which can have an indirect object only; one of these verbs is *to pay*. It would be possible to have such a sentence as *She paid the postman*, in which *the postman* is an indirect object because it indicates to whom payment was made. This sentence could be thought of as an abbreviated form of something like *She paid the postman the necessary amount*, in which *the necessary amount* is the direct object because it is what is paid. Although indirect objects are normally animate, there are a few examples in which the indirect object is inanimate, as in *She gave the room a quick clean*. *The room* is the first of the two objects and so is the indirect object. In such cases it is not really possible to replace the indirect object with a prepositional phrase; we do not accept *She gave a quick clean to the room* as idiomatic.

Some verbs take an indirect object in the prepositional-phrase form. A sentence such as *They delivered the message to the general* cannot be expressed as *They delivered the general the message*. Because of this some scholars have suggested that the prepositional phrase should not be considered as an indirect object at all. But this seems unnecessary since there is such a close correlation between the two types, as many examples in this chapter show; and both forms have normally been considered as indirect objects. Both direct and indirect objects may be made the subject of passive sentences. We have already had the example of *He killed the king* being turned into the passive form *The king was killed by him*, in which the direct object in the first sentence becomes the subject in the second. Where a sentence has both a direct and an indirect object, either may be made the subject of a passive sentence, as in the following examples:

1   They gave the general the message.
2   The general was given the message.
3   The message was given to the general.

In the first sentence the subject is *they*, the predicator is *gave*, the indirect object is *the general*, and the direct object is *the message*. In the second sentence *the general*, which was the indirect object in the first one, is now made the subject. Although this sentence is passive in form it still has an object, because the direct object of the first sentence, *the message*, remains as a direct object in the second. In the third sentence this direct object from the first two sentences is now made the subject. The indirect object in these passive sentences always appears as a prepositional phrase. Although both passive forms are possible, the type with the indirect object converted into the subject is much more common than the type with the direct object converted into the subject. The reason for this is not clear, but it may have something to do with the fact that the indirect object is almost always animate. A major reason for turning an active sentence into a passive one is to turn the focus onto one of the objects. The focus is more likely to be directed at an animate than at an inanimate object. In active sentences where both direct and indirect objects are animate, it is more difficult to say which might be the preferred passive form, as in the following three sentences:

1   They gave her the boy.
2   The boy was given to her.
3   She was given the boy.

The second and third examples are equally acceptable.

In the previous paragraph it was pointed out that with some verbs the indirect object always takes the prepositional-phrase form. In such cases it is not possible to make the indirect object the subject of a passive sentence. The example used then was *They delivered the message to the general*. We saw that it was not possible to have the form *They delivered the general the message*. Equally it is impossible to make *the general* the subject of a passive sentence; one simply cannot say *The general was delivered the message*.

Although direct objects may be formed by a clause, this is not true of indirect objects, since they are usually animate and a clause is not a way in which animates are represented. Both direct and indirect objects may be used in questions, though there are some restrictions on indirect objects when the question is made up of a *wh-* word. The statement *She gave him it* may be made into a question by focusing on either the direct or indirect objects. When the direct object is made the focus of the question the resulting sentence will be *What did she give him?* With the indirect object the situation is less clear. The formal form is *To whom did she give it?* but this is not now used very frequently. The most likely form the question would take is *Who did she give it to?* It is not possible to omit the preposition *to* or to represent the indirect object simply by the non-subject pronoun form *whom*. A sentence such as *Whom did she give it?* is not standard English. The same position applies to indirect questions. In relative clauses, as we have seen, it is possible to omit the relative pronoun. In such clauses, where the relative pronoun is an indirect object, the pronoun itself may be deleted, but not the preposition *to*. This accounts for the form of sentences such as *The general I gave the message to fled*. In this sentence the relative clause acts as the qualifier in the noun group *The general I gave the message to*. The qualifier is a clause consisting of the subject *I*, predicator *gave*, direct object *the message*, and indirect object *to [who(m)]*. The pronoun part of the indirect object *who(m)* may be omitted, and usually is, but the preposition *to* may not. In such clauses the indirect object always has the prepositional form, for it is not possible to say *The general whom I gave the message fled.*

Just as the object can have two different forms, so also the complement can have two separate forms. These are known as the SUBJECT COMPLEMENT and the OBJECT COMPLEMENT. The names are self-explanatory since the subject complement is a complement that refers back to the subject of the sentence, and the object complement is a complement that refers back to the direct object of the sentence. The complements we have discussed so far have been those which follow stative verbs, such as *to be*. In the sentence *He is king*, *he* is the subject, *is* the predicator, and *king* the complement. Since *king* refers back to *he*, which is the subject of the sentence, it is a subject complement. The subject complement occupies the same position in the sentence as an object in that it normally comes directly after the predicator. But it is easier to insert an adverb between the predicator and the complement than it is to do so between the predicator and an object. Sentences with complements and an intervening adverb, such as *He is still king* or *He is already king*, are much more acceptable than ones with objects in a similar position, such as *The boy hit again him* or *The girl eats already meat*. An object complement refers to the direct object and so occurs in sentences with a direct object. As a general rule the object complement follows immediately after the direct object. In the sentence *The gift made her happy*, *the gift* is subject, *made* is predicator, *her* is direct object, and *happy* is the object complement. As this example shows, the complement may be an adjective or adjective group, and that distinguishes it from the object, which cannot be an adjective or adjective group. It is important to distinguish between objects and complements. With a subject complement there is likely to be no problem since it follows stative verbs; direct objects follow transitive verbs, which will be dynamic. But object complements occur in sentences with transitive verbs since they refer to direct objects. The difference between complements and objects in those cases where a transitive verb is followed by two noun groups may be recognised in the following way. In those sentences in which the two noun groups refer to different people or things the noun groups will be objects, but in those in which the two noun groups refer to the same person or thing the first will be a direct object and the second an object complement. This can be seen in the following two examples:

1   The teacher made Dorinda the class prefect.
2   The teacher showed Dorinda the class prefect.

In the first sentence *Dorinda* and *the class prefect* refer to the same person, because Dorinda is now the class prefect. In the second sentence *Dorinda* is a separate person from *the class prefect* because she is being shown who the class prefect is. Consequently in the first sentence *Dorinda* is the direct object and *the class prefect* is the object complement; and in the second sentence *Dorinda* is the indirect object and *the class prefect* is the direct object.

If concord is possible, then traditionally it was felt that the complement should agree with the subject or object to which it refers. Today such concord concerns only pronouns, which are the words with non-subject forms. But, as we have seen, this concord is often avoided, so that forms such as *It's me* and *It's them* are used instead of *It's I* and *It's they*. Subject complements occur with stative verbs, and since those verbs do not have a passive form the subject complement cannot be made the subject of a passive sentence. In principle it should be possible to alter the position of the subject and the subject complement so that *Mr Reagan is the President* could be *The President is Mr Reagan*. This alternation is not possible with all stative verbs. The object complement refers to objects which occur with transitive verbs, and transitive verbs have a passive form. But object complements themselves cannot be made the subject of a passive sentence, even though the objects to which they refer can. In the sentence *The teacher made Dorinda the class prefect*, *Dorinda* is the direct object and *the class prefect* the object complement. The object can be made the subject of a passive sentence to give *Dorinda was made the class prefect by the teacher*; but the object complement cannot be made the subject of a sentence. When the direct object is turned into the subject of a passive sentence as in *Dorinda was made the class prefect by the teacher, the class prefect,* which had been the object complement in the original sentence, is now the subject complement, for it refers to the subject. That is to say that *the class prefect* always refers to *Dorinda,* but, as in the first sentence *Dorinda* was the direct object and in the second the subject, the function of *the class prefect* changes from object complement to subject complement to reflect the change in function of *Dorinda.*

The ADJUNCT, which is the final sentence element, is the one which is most difficult to characterise since it has so many diverse functions and forms. It is perhaps most satisfactory to characterise it in a negative way by stating that anything which is not a subject, predicator, object or complement will be an adjunct. An adjunct, like an adverb, answers questions such as 'Where?', 'When?' and 'How?', and it is more often than not an optional element in a clause. In other words, most clauses would make complete sense if the adjunct were omitted: to omit the adjunct *downstairs* in the sentence *The girl slept downstairs* would still leave a grammatical sentence, *The girl slept.* Because it is an optional element, the adjunct also has much greater freedom of position in its clause than the other clause elements. The most usual position of the adjunct is at the beginning or end of a clause; it may occur between subject and predicator or between predicator and subject complement, but these positions are less common. It rarely appears in other positions. The adjunct can have a variety of different forms: noun group, adverb group, prepositional phrase or clause. Much of what has been written in earlier chapters about the adverb or the adverb group applies to the adjunct, and consequently little more needs to be said here about it.

It is, however, time to consider the employment of one clause as an element in another clause. As we have seen in this chapter, a subject, a direct object or an adjunct may be represented by a clause. This may be illustrated by the following sentences:

1   Clause as subject: *The subject comes before the predicator in declarative sentences* is a rule of standard English.

2　Clause as direct object:　He claimed *that the subject did not come before the predicator in declarative sentences in English.*

3　Clause as adjunct:　*When the subject comes before the predicator,* the sentence is declarative in English.

The parts of the sentences in italics are clauses within a larger sentence. As clauses they each contain at least a subject and a predicator, but they may also contain other clause elements. When a clause is a sentence element such as adjunct, it is called a SUBORDINATE CLAUSE. Subordinate clauses which are adjuncts are easily recognisable, since they are introduced by a subordinating conjunction, as is true of the third example above, where the subordinate clause *When the subject comes before the predicator* is introduced by the conjunction *when*. Subordinate clauses acting as adjuncts are always incomplete sentences, though they may in dialogue act as complete sentences through ellipsis of the rest of the sentence. Thus the question *When did he telephone the butcher?* could have the answer *When he came home* as a complete utterance. But this answer is an elided form of *When he came home he telephoned the butcher*. Clauses acting as subject or direct object may be introduced by a conjunction such as *that*, but need not be. If they are not introduced by a conjunction, they could act as complete sentences. In the first example above, it is perfectly possible to imagine a sentence which reads *The subject comes before the predicator in declarative sentences*. However, it is usually possible to see whether a clause is the subject of a sentence by converting it into a noun group. Thus *The subject comes before the predicator in declarative sentences is a rule of standard English* could be rewritten as *The positioning of the subject before the predicator in declarative sentences is a rule of standard English*. This has *The positioning of the subject before the predicator in declarative sentences* as a noun group, with determiner *the*, head *positioning*, and qualifier *of the subject before the predicator in declarative sentences*.

The opposite of a subordinate clause is the MAIN CLAUSE, which embodies the primary meaning of the sentence. It forms the main structure upon which all the elements in a sentence depend. If there is only one finite verb, that will form the predicator of the main clause. Other clauses will be either subordinate to or co-ordinate with the main clause. If a clause fulfils the function of subject, direct object or adjunct, then it is a subordinate clause. Usually, but not invariably, it is introduced by a subordinating conjunction. Sentences with at least one subordinate clause are known as COMPLEX sentences. Two clauses in a sentence may both be main clauses if they are linked together by a co-ordinating conjunction such as *and* or *but*. The sentence *The alarm sounded and the children got up* consists of two main clauses linked by *and*. Either of the two clauses could stand alone. Sentences with two or more main clauses are known as COMPOUND sentences. Frequently, of course, compound sentences show some form of elision. *The children got up and ate their breakfast* could be said to consist of two main clauses *The children got up* and *The children ate their breakfast*. As the subject is identical in both sentences, the second occurrence may be elided when the two are joined together in a compound sentence. The same information can be arranged in a variety of different ways: as two independent sentences, as a compound sentence, or as a complex sentence. Consider the following examples:

1   Fighting broke out on the terraces. The referee brought the players off the field.
2   Fighting broke out on the terraces and the referee brought the players off the field.
3   When fighting broke out on the terraces, the referee brought the players off the field.

Example 1 contains two sentences; example 2 a compound sentence consisting of two main clauses; and example 3 a complex sentence with a subordinate clause acting as adjunct and a main clause. The decision as to which of the forms to use is largely a stylistic matter, though it is important to recognise the differences among them.

In the chapter on verbs it was pointed out that there is a difference between finite and non-finite verbs. This distinction is important because it is accepted that in standard written English clauses must contain a finite verb. The non-finite parts of the verb, which include participles and infinitives may be employed as noun groups, as in the proverbial utterance *Seeing is believing*. But these non-finite parts of the verb cannot be employed as the predicator of a main clause: *I seeing him* is not an acceptable sentence in standard English. They can, however, be used in a way that resembles subordinate clauses. In the last paragraph there were three examples of how the same idea could be expressed in different grammatical structures. A fourth way is possible. Instead of saying *When fighting broke out on the terraces, the referee brought the players off the field*, it would be possible to say *Fighting breaking out on the terraces, the referee brought the players off the field*. Here the expression *Fighting breaking out on the terraces* occupies the same function as *When fighting broke out on the terraces*. In the first example there is a finite verb *broke*, but in the second a non-finite verb *breaking*. Normally this type of construction with a non-finite verb is referred to as a PARTICIPIAL CONSTRUCTION. Participial constructions are of two types: ABSOLUTE and MODIFYING. In the sentence *Fighting breaking out on the terraces, the referee brought the players off the field*, the participle *breaking* refers to something within the participial construction, namely *fighting*. It does not refer to anything outside the participial construction. It is said to be absolute, because its grammatical frame of reference is restricted within its own construction; it is to that extent self-referring. This example may be contrasted with the sentence *Urging the players to follow, the referee left the field*. In this case there is a participial construction *urging the players to follow*, in which *urging* is a present participle. But *urging* refers to *the referee* – that is, it refers to something which is outside the boundary of the immediate participial construction. *Urging* acts as a form of modifier to *referee*, and so the participial construction is described as a modifying participial construction.

Within the framework of traditional grammar, the make-up of these participial constructions is readily analysable at word level. But it is more difficult to decide whether they should be thought of as clauses or not. Earlier in this chapter it was indicated that a clause could be defined as a unit of language containing a finite verb. Naturally participial constructions do not contain a finite verb, since participles are non-finite. Yet from a structural point of view many participial constructions appear to occupy the same role as that filled by clauses. Consequently in some grammars these constructions are referred to as non-finite clauses. This seems a sensible decision since, although the verbs are non-finite, they still behave in many ways as verbs. In the example *Urging the players to follow, the referee left the field*, the participial construction is *Urging the players to follow*. Although *urging* is a participle, it acts like a verb to the extent that it has an object following it. The players are being urged to do something, and so *the players* is the object of *urging*. In the same way it is the referee who is doing the urging and so *the referee* is like a subject. In other words it is best to accept that there are two kinds of clause: one with a finite verb and the other with a non-finite verb.

The absolute participial construction will act as a clause element such as adjunct or subject, because non-finite clauses will always be subordinate clauses; it is not possible to have a main clause consisting of a non-finite clause. In *Fighting breaking out on the terraces, the referee brought the players off the field*, it may be said that *fighting breaking out on the terraces* is an absolute participial construction which is acting as the adjunct of the main sentence, since it answers the question 'When?' Modifying participial constructions are, as the name implies, part of a noun group, for they modify the head of a noun group which is outside the immediate participial construction. The modifying participial construction does not act by itself as a major sentence element; it forms part of such an element. In the sentence *Urging the players to follow, the referee left the field* the subject is *urging the players to follow, the referee*. *Urging the players to follow* is a modifier within the noun group. It is usually possible, though not always stylistically elegant, to put the modifying participial construction after the head to which it refers: *The referee, urging the players to follow, left the field*. A similar change in position is not usually possible for absolute participial constructions, but they may be placed after the end of the whole main clause rather than in front of it. Indeed in literary texts, and this construction is literary, the final position is perhaps more common than the initial one, for the effect can be cumulative particularly in descriptive passages.

Consider this sentence from *The Adventures of Huckleberry Finn*:

> And then faster and faster they went, all of them dancing, first one foot struck out in the air and then the other, the horses leaning more and more, and the ringmaster going round and round the center pole, cracking his whip and shouting 'Hi! – Hi!' and the clown cracking jokes behind him.

Here there are many examples of the participial construction at the end of the sentence, and it may be noted that some examples use the past participle even though forms with the present participle are more common.

One of the aspects of style which was frequently criticised by older traditional grammarians was the use of a participial construction as though it were absolute, when it really should, in their opinion, have been modifying something outside the construction itself. An example of this is *Realising the problems the legislation was postponed*. Here *realising the problems* is a participial construction in which the *realising* has nothing to which it refers. The writer probably intended it to refer to something like *the cabinet* or *the government* who were responsible for postponing the legislation, but as the main clause has a passive construction no agent responsible for postponing the legislation is mentioned. The *realising the problems* is not an absolute construction as it contains no subject for *realising* within its own boundaries; it should be a modifying participial construction, but the agent to which it refers has been omitted from the main clause. This type of participial construction contains what is sometimes known as a dangling participle, because it dangles by itself without the necessary referent. It is, however, a construction which is not uncommon in all types of writing. Although it is difficult to analyse grammatically, it does not normally cause any ambiguity.

7 Clause Elements and Sentence Types

So far in this book I have dealt with grammar in relation to relatively simple sentences which are statements or declarative sentences. In this chapter we shall consider other types of sentence. But before that we must look at the various ways in which the clause elements can be combined in a declarative sentence. As was pointed out in the last chapter, the elements in a clause are subject, predicator, object, complement and adjunct, and it is these elements which can be regrouped either to vary the style or to indicate different sentence types.

In DECLARATIVE sentences two elements always appear, subject and predicator, and these two occupy the first and second positions in the vast majority of these sentences. The minimal declarative sentence consists of subject and predicator, as in *They have arrived*. In this sentence the verb is intransitive, and it is the nature of the verb which largely determines what other elements will be found within any clause. A transitive verb must have an object after it, and so that type of verb will produce a minimal clause structure of subject–predicator–object. An example of this type of structure is *She hit him*. A stative verb, on the other hand, will be followed by a complement or an adjunct, as in the two examples *She is queen* and *She is there*. Other verbs take two objects or an object and a complement, as in *They gave him the message* and *They made him king*. In these two types the order is respectively subject–predicator–object–object, and subject–predicator–object–complement. Finally some verbs may need an adjunct as well as an object to form a complete clause, as in *You may put the book on the table*, for it would not be sufficient to say only *You may put the book*. In this type of sentence the order of the elements is subject–predicator–object–adjunct.

By using the abbreviations S (subject), P (predicator), O (object), C (complement), and A (adjunct), these various types of clause arrangement may be tabulated as follows:

1   SP   They have arrived.
2   SPO   She hit him.
3   SPC   She is queen.
4   SPA   She is there.
5   SPOO   They gave him the message.
6   SPOC   They made him king.
7   SPOA   You may put the book on the table.

It should be stressed that these orders represent the minimal structures of clause arrangements for declarative sentences in English. Naturally they may be expanded by the introduction of other elements, but these other elements should be considered optional, rather than obligatory, additions. All declarative sentences in English are reducible to one of the structures listed above. Elaboration in English style comes through the expansion of these basic structures. It should also be stated that for the sake of emphasis or style the order of some of these basic structures may be disrupted, but when that happens it will always be understood to embody a departure from the norm. Some of these points will need to be elaborated.

As will be clear from the previous chapters, the individual sentence elements represent a variety of different actual realisations. A predicator can be an active or a passive verb, a stative or a dynamic verb, a transitive or an intransitive verb. Similarly an object may be a direct or an indirect object. So at first sight some sentences may seem to be very different, but on analysis they can be shown to have the same structure. Take the following sentences:

1   She hit him.
2   The message was given to the general.

In the first sentence the predicator is an active transitive verb, *hit*, which is followed by a direct object, *him*. The second sentence, however, has a predicator which is a passive transitive verb, *was given*, with an indirect object, *to the general*. Both sentences may be reduced to the same basic structure, which is SPO. Although the basic structures can be realised in a variety of different ways, this in no way detracts from the similarity of that underlying structure.

Other clause elements can be added to the basic structure of any clause. With the elements S, P, C and O, this means usually that another S or another P can be added within a clause. In other words, a second example of the element will be added and linked to the first through a co-ordinating conjunction. An example of this is *The lecturers from all universities and the students of London University joined in the demonstration against the cuts*. In this sentence there are two subjects linked by *and*, namely *The lecturers from all universities* and *the students of London University*. The two subjects form two noun groups, each with its own head. This is, however, an expansion, rather than a modification, of the basic structure. Because the adjunct is an optional element that can be added freely to many of the basic structures, the sentences listed above could readily be expanded by the addition of one or more adjuncts:

1   They have arrived *already*.
2   She hit him *with the rolling pin*.
3   She is queen *now*.
4   She is there *today*.
5   They gave him the message *immediately*.
6   They made him king *on his father's death*.
5   You may put the book on the table *when you are ready*.

Adjuncts of time and place are probably the ones which are most commonly found and they are usually added at the end of the clause. They may be added in other positions, because the adjunct as an optional element has a much freer position. This movement of the adjunct may be considered with the repositioning of the other clause elements, since variation from the basic order is largely a matter of style.

English is not an inflected language; that is to say that it does not have, for example, endings to the nouns which indicate that a noun with one ending is the subject and a noun with another ending is the object. Nouns used to have a system of endings in earlier English, and some idea of what that was like may be gained from a consideration of the pronouns which still distinguish between such forms as the subject *I* and the non-subject *me*. Because nouns do not have any endings to indicate function, word order in English is of great importance in determining which word is the subject and which the object and in indicating whether a particular sentence is declarative or not. This means that there is a limit to the amount of movement which can take place in the basic elements of a clause if ambiguity is to be prevented. On the other hand, since the subject is normally the first element to occur in any clause, the filling of that first position by any other element will cause it to have emphasis because it will occur in an unexpected order. We can appreciate this in a sentence such as *The wine he took; the food he left on the table.* In the first clause the subject is *he*, because *he* is doing the action of the verb *took*. What is taken is *the wine*, which must be the object of the clause. The normal order of this type of sentence is SPO, but in this clause it has become OSP and it has thrown *the wine* into considerable emphasis. The form *He took the wine* is much less forceful than *The wine he took*. This example represents a severe dislocation of the normal order and it results in *The wine* having considerable stress. In the spoken language this kind of emphasis can be achieved through stress and intonation patterns, but in writing it has to be done through word order. The same applies to adjuncts, but there the emphasis may be said to be less powerful. The expected order when an adjunct is included might be *He took the wine yesterday*, which could be rearranged as *Yesterday he took the wine*. The latter example puts *yesterday* into a prominent position, but as the adjunct is not part of the basic structure of this clause its emphasis when placed first is not so strong as that on *the wine* when it comes in the initial position. It is only the first element in the sentence which carries the stress and so it would not be normal to have a sentence such as *Yesterday the wine he took*, with two elements out of their expected order, since *the wine* would not occupy first position and so would not have the stress which was intended for it. This type of sentence would seem merely fussy.

A declarative sentence is one which embodies a statement and it can be recognised because the subject precedes the predicator. Two other types of sentence are those which ask questions and are known as INTERROGATIVE sentences, and those which embody commands and are known as IMPERATIVE sentences. Interrogative sentences resemble declaratives in that both have subject and predicator, but in interrogative sentences their order is reversed. Imperative sentences differ from both these types in that they do not contain a subject at all. The three types may be distinguished schematically in this way:

> Declarative   SP . . .
> Interrogative PS . . .
> Imperative   P . . .

The dots indicate the other clause elements which may follow in each case. The basic clause structures which were given for declarative sentences earlier in this chapter also apply to the other sentence types, except that interrogatives will have subject and predicator reversed in order and imperatives will have no subject. The particular examples given may not be readily transformed into other sentence types, but it is not difficult to find comparable examples. The first example, *They have arrived*, consists of subject and predicator, which is formed of an intransitive verb. The interrogative equivalent is simply *Have they arrived?*, in which the subject no longer occupies the first position but has been placed after the auxiliary *have*. An imperative equivalent of this sentence is hardly possible, since imperatives are not found in the past tense and since *arrive* is not usually used as a command. But similar intransitive verbs may be used as commands, such as *come* and *go*.

Although all interrogative verbs have inversion of subject and predicator, this inversion takes a rather special form, as the example *Have they arrived?* from the previous paragraph indicates. In that sentence the predicator is a verb group consisting of auxiliary and head. When the subject and predicator are reversed in order, it is only the auxiliary part of the verb group which is placed before the subject. The form of the interrogative is *Have they arrived?* and not *Have arrived they?* When the equivalent declarative sentence has no auxiliary, as in *They arrived yesterday*, then it is necessary to include an auxiliary when that type of declarative is transformed into an interrogative. The auxiliary which is added in such cases is a part of *do*. Hence to change *They arrived yesterday* into a question, one must also include a part of the auxiliary *do* to give the interrogative *Did they arrive yesterday?* The addition of a form of *do* does not apply to sentences whose predicators are made up of a part of the verb *to be*. In these cases the predicator and the verb are reversed and there is no additional auxiliary. The interrogative form of the declaratives *She is queen* and *She is there* is *Is she queen?* and *Is she there?* respectively.

There are two main types of interrogative sentence: one which expects an answer which is either *yes* or *no*, and the other which expects as a reply something other than a simple *yes* or *no*. In the first category the interrogative sentence is arranged in the order outlined in the previous paragraph, for all the examples given there expect either *yes* or *no* as an answer. Questions such as *Did they arrive yesterday?* or *Is she queen?* can be answered by a simple *yes* or *no*, though naturally some speakers may not reply in such a straightforward manner. The important consideration is that a *yes* or *no* would be a sufficient answer to such questions. Other questions are not like this, for they allow for a wide range of possible replies. These other questions are introduced by an interrogative word such as *what?*, *which?* or *how?*, but the structure of the clause will still be interrogative in that the subject will come after the auxiliary part of the predicator. *What did you have for breakfast?* is an example of this type of interrogative construction. The answer to this type of question can never be a simple *yes* or *no*, and the range of potential answers is very large. Interrogatives of this kind are often referred to as *wh-* questions because they are introduced by an interrogative word, and most such words start with *wh*. But the basic structure of the sentence is interrogative, with the auxiliary *did* before the subject *you*, which is followed in turn by the head of the verb group *have*.

It is possible to think of a third type of interrogative sentence which consists of an amalgamation of two or more *yes–no* questions to form what might be called an *either–or* question. Let us start with the *yes–no* question *Are you coming down to breakfast now?* It is possible to add another *yes–no* question to this one so that the person being addressed is presented with alternatives of which he can choose one only in reply. The above question could be expanded to *Are you coming down to breakfast now or are you going to stay in bed all day?* Although each half of this question is a *yes–no* one, together they present the question in such a way that a simple *yes–no* answer is no longer possible. But from a structure point of view these questions do not differ from ordinary *yes–no* questions.

Although I have drawn a clear distinction between the SP order of declarative sentences and the PS order of interrogative ones, there are occasions when this order is violated. Throughout the history of English there has been a tendency to put the subject first in a clause, but in the past when a clause began with an adverb it was usual to have the predicator before the subject. One needs only think of Milton's beautiful passage in Book IV of *Paradise Lost* which opens *Now came still evening on* to realise that this was so. Here the adverb *now* is followed directly by the verb *came* to give the order APS. This order may still be found in modern English. It occurs not infrequently in literature, where it provides variety in the style. It is also found rather more in American scholarly writing than it is in its British equivalent. A sentence such as *In this setting becomes intelligible the mooted question of James's assumption of British citizenship a few months before his death** is one which is probably more characteristic of American than of British academic work. In this sentence the subject *the mooted question of James's assumption of British citizenship* is put after the predicator with its complement,

---

* Saul Rosenzweig, 'The Ghost of Henry James' in *Modern Criticism: Theory and Practice*, ed. Walter Sutton and Richard Foster (New York: Odyssey Press, 1963) p. 412.

becomes intelligible. This is because the sentence opens with the adjunct *In this setting*. The positioning of the predicator before the subject is also a feature of some American journalistic styles, such as that found in *Time* magazine, and British imitations. In these journalistic styles the inversion of subject and predicator does not necessarily depend upon the presence of an initial adjunct. Nevertheless, the positioning of the subject after the predicator may be found in less exotic situations than literature or American journalism. Consider the sentence *Dorinda's coming to tea and so am I*. The final clause *so am I* has the order APS. It is not possible to phrase that as *and so I am*. But, if a different adverb is used instead of *so* and if it is placed at the end of the clause, then the normal order of subject and predicator would follow, as in *Dorinda's coming to tea and I am too*. This type of inversion is now restricted to the verbs *to be* and *to have*, and it differs from the inversion found in interrogative sentences in that it does not require the presence of an auxiliary.

For their part interrogative sentences may have an SP order, though this applies only to *yes–no* interrogatives. *Wh*-questions always have SP inversion. In speech a declarative sentence such as *You are coming to tea tomorrow* can be converted into a question simply by altering the stress and intonation pattern. In writing the same effect is achieved by putting a question mark after the sentence to give *You are coming to tea tomorrow?* In many cases it is difficult to decide whether the speaker's intention is to ask a question or to express an exclamation, for it is possible to punctuate the sentence above as *You are coming to tea tomorrow!* Questions which verge towards exclamations and thus hardly expect to receive an answer at all because the question presupposes the answer are known as RHETORICAL QUESTIONS. Interrogative sentences which do not have inversion of subject and predicator are likely to be rhetorical questions.

It is possible to convert a declarative sentence into an interrogative one by adding a tag question to it. A tag usually consists of an auxiliary with a pronoun which refers back to the subject of the clause to which the tag is appended. If there is a declarative sentence such as *Dorinda's not coming*, it is possible to add the tag *is she?* to it. This tag consists of an auxiliary, in this case part of the verb *to be*, and the pronoun *she*, which refers back to the *Dorinda* of the main clause. If the main clause is negative it is followed by a positive tag as in the example given, but if the main clause is positive it is followed by a negative tag. The auxiliary generally repeats the auxiliary of the main clause, so, if the main clause has a part of the verb *to be*, that is reflected in the tag. In the sentence above, the *'s* in *Dorinda's not coming* stands for *is*, so *is* occurs in the tag. The same applies to sentences such as *She has got one* and *She did tell him*, which would have the tags *hasn't she?* and *didn't she?* respectively. If the main clause does not contain an auxiliary, then the tag uses *do* as a kind of dummy auxiliary to replace the verb of the main clause. Thus a clause such as *She understands the importance of the matter* would have the tag *doesn't she?* if one were required. Many tag questions resemble rhetorical questions or exclamations in their conversational implication, for they often presuppose an answer which need not be given. They are also more characteristic of speech than of formal writing, in which exclamations or rhetorical questions are more commonly found. It is, however, possible to have a positive tag with a positive main clause, as in *You are the manager, are you?* but these tags frequently imply some condescension or irony on the part of the speaker. Consequently such tags are not met with that often. It is also possible to reinforce a command by the addition of a tag question which may be either positive or negative irrespective of the polarity of the main clause. These tag questions do not follow the same rules about auxiliaries as other tags, since where the main clause has no auxiliary the tag does not have to use *do*. It may rely on other auxiliaries, and the same command may even have different auxiliaries on different occasions. Thus a command such as *Shut up* could be followed by *will you?*, *won't you?* or *can't you?* These tags reinforce the command they follow and may be regarded as providing emphasis. Tags may also be applied to exclamations and serve there to reinforce the exclamatory force of the sentence. They may be added even to those clauses which have been elided, as in *Awful, isn't it?* The absence of the *It's* in the main clause does not prevent the addition of a tag.

Imperative sentences are of two basic types: those in which the speaker addresses a command to another person or to other people, and those in which he includes himself in the command. The first kind is the more common and it may be characterised as a sentence which has no subject and which has a predicator consisting of a verb in the base form. If there is an auxiliary, which is not very usual, that will occur in the base form. Typical examples of commands are *Come here* and *Go away*. The two predicators *come* and *go* have no subjects before them, and so the predicator will normally appear as the first element of an imperative. The verbs *come* and *go* are in the base form. It is possible to use the auxiliary *do* as part of the predicator of an imperative to give sentences such as *Do come here* or *Do go away*. In modern English forms with *do* may well suggest frustration or pleading on the part of the speaker. Negative imperative sentences, however, must have the auxiliary *do* as part of the predicator, so that the negative equivalents of *Come here* and *Go away* are *Don't come here* and *Don't go away* respectively. The imperative has a verb in the base form, and variation in tenses is not allowed. An imperative which referred to the future would be structured as an interrogative, even if both speaker and hearer understood the interrogative to have the force of a command. Hence a teacher might say to his pupils *Will you hand in your essays tomorrow?*, in which the form is that of a question, but the intention is that of a command. Imperatives do not admit modal auxiliaries in the predicator, and in standard written English they do not usually accept the progressive form of the present tense, though such forms may be found colloquially. A sentence like *Be doing this while I am away*, in which the predicator is *be doing*, may be found in speech, but is unlikely in more formal contexts. It is possible to have a passive form of imperative in which the predicator consists of *be* with a past participle. This type of imperative is much more frequent in negative constructions, as in *Don't be taken in by the advertising*.

In earlier varieties of English imperatives more often than not had a subject, but in modern English, as we have seen, the subject has dropped out. It might be more accurate to say that it has been replaced by a form of address, which may be a personal name or a pronoun, although in some cases it may be difficult to decide whether a subject or a form of address is involved. With a personal name it is almost always a matter of a form of address, which may be described as a VOCATIVE. In writing a vocative will be set off from the command by a comma, and in speech by a pause. In a sentence such as *Jane, go away*, the *Jane* would always be understood as a vocative, intended to arouse the attention of the person addressed, and not as the subject. The same applies fairly regularly to a pronoun, as in *You, come here*. This seems to be the case because the *you* can be qualified by words such as *there*, which is only possible with a vocative. We can say *You there, come here*, but not *You there come here*. However, the situation is complicated because in some circumstances it does seem possible to have a subject with an imperative. Two situations in particular have such a subject: one when the subject of the imperative stands in contrast with another subject, as in *You write the labels and I'll stick them on*; and the other when there is a vocative as well as a subject, as in *Jane, you write the labels*. It would not be possible for this to be punctuated as *Jane you, write the labels*. It is clear that in both cases the imperative has a subject. One must, therefore, conclude that commands addressed solely to other people normally have no subject, though a subject may be included in certain circumstances. However, the chances of confusion with a declarative sentence are not high, because the pronominal subject of this type of command will always be *you* and because *you* and the base form of a dynamic verb do not occur often as subject and predicator of a declarative sentence.

Imperative sentences which include the speaker within the command are introduced by *let*, but the pronoun which refers to the speaker either by himself or in conjunction with others appears in the non-subject form, either *me* or *us*, rather than in the subject form. Thus we have sentences such as *Let me decide what to do* and *Let's go to the station together*. In the second example the *'s* is a shortened form of *us*, and this abbreviated form is characteristic of speech. To turn commands of this type into the negative one can either include *not* after the *let* and the pronoun or begin the clause with *don't* to give either

Let's not go to the station together or *Don't let's go to the station together*. As the speaker is included in this type of command, it follows that the pronouns used will be the first person *me* and *us* in their non-subject form. But a third person pronoun in its non-subject form can be used if it is non-specific in its reference, so that the speaker could be seen to be included within the command. If I say at a meeting *If anyone disagrees with this motion let him say so at once*, the command would be seen to apply to everybody at the meeting, including myself. Although this is so, this type of construction is now becoming somewhat old-fashioned.

In this chapter we have outlined three types of sentence in English: declarative, interrogative and imperative. It is possible to consider a fourth type, which may be called the EXCLAMATIVE sentence. This is one which embodies an exclamation. A sentence of this type is *What a nice wife he's got!* In this sentence the order of the elements is OSP. It is, of course, also possible to have exclamative sentences which have the basic order of declarative sentences, such as *He's got an extremely nice wife!*, which has the normal SPO order. It is for this reason that one may doubt whether the exclamative sentence should be separated out as a separate type of sentence of the same rank as declarative, interrogative and imperative. It may be better to think of it rather as a sub-type of the declarative sentence. In speech exclamatory utterances are marked by intonation and stress; in writing they may be indicated by an exclamation mark or through the rearrangement of the order of the elements by putting the object of a clause first. But this type of re-ordering of clause elements may be undertaken for emphasis or marking rather than to produce some kind of exclamation. Not all sentences which have an OSP order have to be understood as exclamatives. An example quoted earlier in this chapter, *The wine he took; the bread he left on the table*, is an illustration of that. The object has been put into first position for stylistic reasons, and not to turn the sentence into an exclamative. There is thus no specific order which belongs exclusively to exclamative sentences. It is true that some exclamative sentences may have a word indicating an exclamation, such as *what!* or *how!*, to introduce them, as in the example *What a nice wife he's got!* But these words are not essential to produce exclamative sentences, for that example could be expressed *A nice wife he's got!* Indeed, many exclamatory utterances are notable for the fact that they contain some form of elision, so that they may be no more than a word or a group such as *Stupendous!* or *A breathtaking view!* In these cases it is impossible to decide what the order of the clause elements would have been if the speaker had not elided the clause to a word or group. It is therefore right to realise that there are sentences which are exclamative in English, but it is better to think of them as forming a sub-type within the declarative sentence.

Although there is considerable variation within any one type of sentence, it is possible to delimit three major types in English which can be distinguished by the order of their clause elements. These are the declarative sentence, which has an SP order; the interrogative sentence, which has a PS order; and the interrogative, which has no subject and has the predicator as its first element. Within the declarative sentence it is possible to trace a sub-type, the exclamative sentence, which maintains the declarative order of SP but which also frequently puts the object before the SP elements.

8 Clause Types

It was pointed out in an earlier chapter that clauses are of two main types: main and subordinate. The main clause is also known as the superordinate clause since *superordinate* stands in direct contrast with *subordinate*. As the names imply, the main or superordinate clause is the primary structure to which all the words or other clauses stand in a subordinate relationship. The main clause can stand by itself, whereas subordinate clauses cannot usually do so because of their dependence upon the main clause. Subordinate clauses act either as sentence elements of the main clause – that is, they act as subject, object, or adjunct in the main clause – or else they form part of one of the sentence elements by acting, for example, as the qualifier of a noun group which is subject, object or complement of a clause. In very complex sentences it is possible to have one subordinate clause acting as an element of another clause which is itself subordinate to the main clause. Three classes of words can have their functions replaced by a clause – nouns, adjectives and adverbs; and in this chapter the clauses formed from them will be dealt with.

NOUN CLAUSE can act as the subject or object of a clause. As object they most commonly follow certain types of verbs, such as verbs of saying, knowing or doubting, and they act as the direct objects of those verbs. Most fall into two major types: those introduced by *that*, though the *that* can be omitted in many cases; and those introduced by words such as *what, whether* or *how*. If these noun clauses had been main clauses, those in the first category would have been declarative clauses and those in the second either interrogative or exclamative ones. Consider the following examples, in which the noun clauses, all acting as direct object, are italicised:

1   He said *that they were foolish.*
2   He doubted *whether they were at home.*
3   He knows *how truthful you are.*

If these objects were to be converted into main clauses by themselves, they would have become as follows:

1   They are foolish
2   Are they at home?
3   How truthful you are!

The first sentence is a simple declarative, the second an interrogative, and the third an exclamative. The second example represents a *yes–no* question, but it is also possible to have a *wh*-question represented by a noun clause acting as object. In *I don't know why they want to get married*, the direct object is *why they want to get married*, which corresponds to the interrogative sentence *Why do they want to get married?* and that is a *wh*-question.

It may be appreciated from examples 1 and 2 above that, when a main clause is converted into a subordinate noun clause acting as object in a different main clause, certain changes occur in its structure. These changes are very closely associated with what are known as DIRECT and INDIRECT SPEECH, partly because so many of the verbs which can take a noun clause as direct object refer to speaking. Consider the following two clauses:

He said, 'I am foolish.'
He said that he was foolish.

Direct speech is indicated in English by the use of single or double inverted commas, and both the clause indicating the action of speaking and the clause representing what was said may be regarded as main clauses even though they are not linked by a co-ordinate conjunction. There is great freedom in the positioning of the *he said* clause, which can even be omitted altogether. The following possibilities are available:

1   He said, 'I am foolish.'

2   'I am foolish', he said.
3   'I', he said, 'am foolish.'
4   'I am foolish.'

It is the last example in which *he said* is omitted that indicates we are here dealing with two main clauses. What is in inverted commas is direct speech and forms an independent clause, and clauses such as *he said* are simply used to set the scene or to act as introductory markers.

When direct speech is put into indirect speech, the relationship of the two clauses noted in the last paragraph changes. When *He said, 'I am foolish'* becomes *He said that he was foolish*, there is a change from two main clauses to a main and a subordinate clause. In *He said that he was foolish*, the *that he was foolish* is a subordinate clause which is a noun clause acting as direct object to *said*. This tighter relationship is indicated by the inability to move *He said* to a different position in the sentence or to leave it out. Sentences such as the following, which correspond to the direct-speech examples noted above, are not acceptable in modern standard English:

1   That he was foolish, he said.
2   That, he said, he was foolish.
3   That he was foolish.

Because the noun clause acts as the object of *said*, the normal rules governing the position of sentence elements operate and there is a tight restriction on the position of those elements. The regular SPO order dictates their position in this case. This restriction on order does not apply to two main clauses, which are characteristic of direct speech, since the order of one clause need have no bearing on the positioning of elements in another main clause or on the order of one clause relative to the other.

In addition to this change in the relationship between the two clauses some parts of the clause in direct speech are changed when that is converted into indirect speech. Firstly, all pronouns and possessive adjectives are put into the third person. In the earlier example *I* becomes *he*. This can lead to uncertainty as to the referent of the pronominal subject in the subordinate clause. The sentence with indirect speech *He said that he was foolish* does in fact have two possible direct speech equivalents, which are *He said, 'I am foolish'* and *He said, 'He is foolish.'* In indirect speech the subject of the subordinate clause may refer back to the subject of the main clause or to someone else. Secondly, adverbs, pronouns and adjectives are changed from those which refer to present time or to proximity in space to those which indicate past time or distance. Hence *now* is changed to *then, here* to *there,* and *this* and *these* to *that* and *those.* Finally, the verbs are also transformed one stage further back in the time sequence so that, for example, verbs in the present become preterite and those in the preterite become pluperfect. This change is illustrated in the appearance of *was* for *is* in the example quoted earlier. These changes illustrate that what was said took place some time in the past and are now being referred to by someone else. It is for this reason that most of these changes occur, for the speaker and the focus of the talk are changed.

These changes operate only when one person is reporting what another person has said; they presuppose that what is said has no direct reference to whoever is reporting it. If, however, the person reporting what was said is referring to what he himself has said earlier or what someone else has said about him, then either the changes are not introduced at all or they occur to a reduced extent. Consider the following pairs of sentences:

1a   He said, 'You are foolish.'
1b   He said that I was foolish.
2a   I said, 'I am silly to do this.'
2b   I said that I was silly to do that.

In sentence 1b the speaker of the main clause is the *I* of the subordinate clause, who is reporting what someone else said about him. The focus is therefore his own point of view. But in 1a, which is the direct-speech equivalent of 1b, he must report what the speaker said in direct speech, and so the focus of the direct speech is that of the subject of the main verb, who would use *you* about the speaker in his own speech.

In both 2a and 2b the focus is the same, since the person reporting the speech and the speaker are the same person. Nevertheless, the relationship between the clauses in each pair of clauses remains the same as that applying in all cases of direct and indirect speech. Sentences 1a and 2a contain two main clauses, while sentences 1b and 2b contain a main and a subordinate clause. In these cases the subordinate clause is the direct object of the verb in the main clause.

Some direct objects which are noun clauses can be introduced by *what* or *whatever*, which have the meaning 'that which' and so introduce a noun clause with a relative function. In *I understand what you are saying* and *The burglar took whatever he could find of value*, the direct objects are *what you are saying* and *whatever he could find of value*. These are both noun clauses in which *what* and *whatever* are the direct objects of *are saying* and *could find* respectively. An object introduced by *whatever* may be placed at the beginning of the main clause, so that the second example could appear as *Whatever he could find of value the burglar took*.

In an earlier chapter we saw that, beside ordinary clauses which contain a finite verb, there are non-finite noun clauses which have a non-finite verb. These clauses contain either a participle or an infinitive. The participle is either a present participle ending in *-ing* or a past participle ending in *-ed*, *-(e)n* or one of the other, less common endings. An infinitive consists either of the base form of the verb by itself or of the base form preceded by *to*. Non-finite clauses composed either of a participle or of an infinitive can occur as the direct object of a clause. Which non-finite part of the verb is used may depend upon the predicator in the main clause, as can be illustrated by the following examples:

1 Dorinda enjoys *telling funny stories*.
2 Dorinda likes *to tell funny stories*.

In each example the direct object is italicised. Each object is a non-finite clause, which consists of the non-finite verb, the participle *telling* in one case and the infinitive *to tell* in the other; and the object of that non-finite verb, which is *funny stories* in both cases. The choice between the participle *telling* and the infinitive *to tell* depends on the verb which precedes. *Enjoy* can be followed only by a participle, but *like* may have either a participle or an infinitive after it. The subject of these non-finite clauses is *Dorinda*, for it is she who tells the stories. It could be said that the first sentence is a shorthand way of saying *Dorinda enjoys that Dorinda tells funny stories*, though that is not how this idea is expressed in English. It is possible for the subject of the non-finite clause to be different from the subject of the main clause. The second example could be changed to *Dorinda likes her daddy to tell funny stories*, in which *her daddy* is the subject of *to tell*, and *her daddy to tell funny stories* is the direct object of the main clause which has *Dorinda* as subject and *likes* as predicator.

I have started by considering noun clauses when used as direct objects because they are most easily recognised in that position, as they occur most often there. They can also occur as subject. In this function noun clauses appear in the same varieties as they do in the object function, but they occur in some cases less frequently. It is possible to have a noun clause as subject introduced by *that*, but it is less common than its equivalent as object and continues to decrease in popularity. One no longer expects to meet such sentences as *That the government has slumped in popularity is clear to everyone*, since this type of sentence is regarded as somewhat pompous. The idea would usually be expressed with a dummy subject and the noun clause at the end: *It is clear to everyone that the government has slumped in popularity*. In this sentence there is a dummy subject *it* and a delayed subject, *that the government has slumped in popularity*, which stands in apposition to that subject as a kind of delayed qualifier and expands it. When the idea of a fall in government popularity is wanted at the beginning of the sentence so that it has greater emphasis, then it is more likely to be expressed as a noun group than as a noun clause: *The slump in government popularity is clear to everyone*. Noun clauses introduced by *what*, *whether* and suchlike words can act as the subject of the main clause, though those introduced by *how* will normally appear with a dummy subject. The following examples illustrate this range of structures.

1 *Whether the tenant can be evicted* depends on his behaviour.
2 *What he already knows* is uncertain.
3 *It* is very frustrating *how she goes on.*

Each subject is italicised, and in the last example the dummy subject anticipates the real subject, which is placed at the end of the sentence. It is also quite possible to have non-finite noun clauses as subject, as in *Reading books is the best way to spend an evening* and *To die for one's country is the highest expression of patriotism.* In these sentences the non-finite noun clauses acting as subject are *Reading books* and *To die for one's country.* Neither of these clauses has an independent subject, and the occurrence of a subject in clauses of this type is not very frequent and is governed by certain restrictions. With a *to*-infinitive the subject will usually be preceded by *for*, as in *For the government to act in that way is very shortsighted.* It would not be idiomatic to omit the initial *for* in the non-finite clause, which in this example is *For the government to act in that way*, in which *the government* functions as a subject of the predicator *to act*, which is an infinitive. When a present participle has a pronoun subject the trend is to make that subject into a possessive pronoun, whereas traditionally and sometimes still colloquially the non-subject form of the pronoun is used. Thus instead of *Him getting angry spoiled the party*, it is now usual to have *His getting angry spoiled the party*, which has the effect of converting the participle into the head of a noun group. Even so it still retains its verbal qualities, since the participle can still have its own object, as in *His teasing the cat was the first sign of his depravity.* In this case *His teasing the cat* is the noun clause acting as subject, and it consists of *his*, which is a determiner but acts as a quasi-subject to *teasing*; *teasing* itself, which is a noun but which still retains some of its verbal force as though it was a predicator; and *the cat*, which is the object of the predicator *teasing.* The uncertainty as to the status of the initial pronoun is reflected in those cases where the non-finite clause has a noun rather than a pronoun as subject. In the sentence *The student teasing the cat led to his expulsion*, one might have expected *the student* to appear as *the student's* so that it would be a possessive like *his.* But today the form with *'s* is very rarely found in this kind of example, and so *the student* has to be understood as a subject of the non-finite clause.

ADJECTIVE CLAUSES are essentially restricted to relative clauses, which normally function as the qualifier of a noun group. Although an adjective comes before the head of a noun group, because single words such as individual adjectives can act only as modifiers, this situation cannot apply in the case of an adjective clause, since the single-word adjective is replaced by a multi-word clause. Within the noun group single words come before the head, but units of several words come after it. So an adjective will occupy the modifier slot, but an adjective clause will occupy the qualifier position. Relative clauses may be introduced by the relative pronouns *who*, *which* and *that*, but these pronouns may be omitted under certain conditions. *Who* refers back to human antecedents, *which* to non-human ones, and *that* to either. *Who* has a non-subject form *whom*, though this is not much used any more, and a possessive *whose*. The form *whose* is sometimes used for non-human antecedents to avoid having to employ the clumsy *of which*. The relative pronoun can function as subject or object of the adjective clause in addition to indicating possession. It is when it is functioning as the object of the adjective clause that it can be omitted, and in speech it more often is than not. Consider the following examples:

1   The boy *who does the garden* has broken his leg.
2   The boy *[who(m)] you caught in the garden* has broken his leg.
3   The boy *[who(m)] you gave sixpence to* has broken his leg.
4   The boy *whose ball keeps landing in our garden* has broken his leg.

In sentence 1 *who does the garden* is the adjectival clause, which contains *who* as subject, *does* as predicator, and *the garden* as direct object. In standard written English *who* cannot be omitted in this position, but in speech it often is, particularly after *there is*, *it is* and similar expressions. *There's somebody wants to come in* may be heard frequently in speech, but it is not acceptable in more formal varieties of the language. In sentence 2 *who(m)* is the direct object of *caught*, which has *you* as its subject, and, as the square brackets indicate, this non-subject form may be omitted. In sentence 3 *who(m)* is the indirect object of the adjective clause, which has *you* as subject, *gave* as predicator, and *sixpence* as direct object. It too as a non-subject form may be omitted. In sentence 4 *whose ball* is the subject of the adjective clause and the subject is a noun group in which the possessive *whose* is a determiner. In the first three sentences *that* could be used instead of *who* or *whom. Which*, and to a lesser extent *who(m)*, may be governed by a preposition and this form was common in older varieties of the language, such as that of the Authorised Version of the Bible. Today *which* or *that* is frequently omitted and the preposition may also be left out. The sentence *Show him the way we came* stands for something like *Show him the way by which we came* or *Show him the way that we came on*. But the prepositional phrases *by which* and *that . . . on* which mark out the relative clause are left out, and this applies now as much to written as to spoken English.

There are two types of relative clause, restrictive and non-restrictive. The first type restricts the interpretation of the head of the noun group by indicating it refers only to the category indicated by the adjective clause. In written language this type of relative is not marked off by commas and in spoken language it is not preceded and followed by a pause. Hence in the sentence *Students who have failed their exam must see the professor immediately* the adjective clause *who have failed their exam* acts as a qualifier to the head *students* and restricts its meaning, for it is not all students who must see the professor, but only those who have failed their exam. The second type does not restrict the interpretation of the head in this way, but adds information about the head which may be assumed to apply to all people or things indicated by the head. Non-restrictive relatives are normally marked off by commas in writing and by pauses in speech. The sentence *Students, who are noted for their laziness, should not be supported by the state* indicates that all students are noted for their laziness and that no student should be supported by the state. If this sentence were to be rewritten as *Students who are noted for their laziness should not be supported by the state*, then it would mean that only

those students who were noted for their laziness should not be financially supported. It would indicate that students fall into two categories: those who are lazy and those who are not.

One type of adjective clause which is found more characteristically in speech and so is somewhat frowned upon in the written language is that which has no specific antecedent since it refers to the preceding clause as a whole rather than to the head of a noun group. In the sentence *Jane is a pretty resilient girl, which is just as well* the adjective clause is *which is just as well*. But that refers back not so much to *a resilient girl* as to the sense of the clause as a whole, i.e. the fact that she is a resilient girl. That this is so is made clear by the particular relative pronoun, for a human antecedent such as *girl* would normally be followed by *who*, and it is only non-animate antecedents, including abstract concepts, which are followed by *which*. In some cases a new head for the relative clause can be added after the main clause and that provides an encapsulation of the meaning of the preceding clause. This can be seen in *Jane is a pretty stupid girl, a fact we cannot ignore*. Here the adjective clause *we cannot ignore* relates directly to *a fact*, which itself summarises what the preceding clause indicates.

There are many types of ADVERB CLAUSE and this multiplicity reflects the various roles which adverbs can play in English. Adverbs can be identified because they answer such questions as 'When?', 'How?' and 'Where?', and adverb clauses fulfil the same function. They may be categorised by the role they occupy. For example, those that answer the question 'When?' may be thought of as adverb clauses of time. Each adverbial clause is normally introduced by a subordinating conjunction, though there may be more than one conjunction which could introduce any one type of adverb clause. Adverb clauses of time, for example, may be introduced by *when, after, before, until, till* and several other conjunctions. Some conjunctions may consist of more than one word and sometimes these words may be distributed partly in the main clause and partly in the subordinate clause. In such cases it is better to analyse the word(s) in the main clause as an adverb and the word(s) introducing the

subordinate clause as a conjunction. In the sentence *No sooner had Dorinda left than the party broke up* it is clear that there is a close relation between *no sooner* and *than*. Here there is a time sequence in which one action happens immediately before another. But it will be appreciated from this example that it is difficult to keep the functions of adverb clauses entirely separate, because there is not only a temporal relationship between the subordinate and main clause, but also a causal relationship, since it is implied that the party broke up because Dorinda left. In the sentence the first clause is subordinate and the second is main, and this can be seen from the possible ways in which it could be rewritten: *When Dorinda left, the party broke up*; *As soon as Dorinda left, the party broke up*; and even *Because Dorinda left, the party broke up*. This last example stresses the causal rather than the temporal relationship between the actions. The clauses which have been referred to so far are those which contain a finite verb. It is also possible to use non-finite clauses in the adverbial function, and in some cases a non-finite clause is regular, if not obligatory. Adverb clauses of time which refer to the future are frequently expressed with an infinitive rather than with a finite verb, for the latter seems rather pedantic to many speakers of the language. Hence *I am waiting for him to come* may appear less clumsy than *I am waiting until he comes*, though it could be argued that the sense of purpose is rather more apparent in the first than in the second example, which because it is less common may now be regarded as somewhat more emphatic.

Adverb clauses of time may refer to any aspect of time in relation to that indicated by the main clause: it may be before, at the same time as, or after, as well as indicating either habitual action or contingency. The relationship implied will dictate the subordinating conjunction which is used. Time past is indicated by conjunctions such as *when* or *after*, whereas time before uses *before*. Habitual action is indicated by *whenever*. The sequence of time involved is that with time-before clauses the action of the main clause takes place before that in the subordinate one, and with time-after clauses the action in the main clause takes place after that in the subordinate one. In the sentence *He wrote fifteen books*

before he was made a professor, there is a subordinate adverb clause of time *before he was made a professor*. The action in this subordinate clause follows that indicated in the main clause, i.e. first he wrote fifteen books and then subsequently he was made a professor. The idea in this sentence can be expressed in a time-after clause, but then the sentence will be rewritten as follows: *He was made a professor after he had written fifteen books*. In this example there is a subordinate adverb clause of time *after he had written fifteen books*. This adverb clause refers to an action which took place before that in the main clause. In order to maintain the proper sequence of events, what had been the main clause in the time-before sentence has to be made into the subordinate clause in the time-after sentence. Which of the two sentence types is chosen will reflect the focus and emphasis the writer wishes to imprint on the idea in the sentence. Both these sentences could be expressed with non-finite rather than with finite adverb clauses: *He wrote fifteen books before being made a professor*, and *He was made a professor after writing fifteen books*.

Adverb clauses of place are normally introduced by *where*, though place can be implied by some other conjunctions. In *Where there had once been green fields there were hideous factories* there is an adverb clause of place *where there had once been green fields*. Place can be implied by some conjunctions which are otherwise used of time, such as *when*. In the sentence *When you get to the top of the hill, turn right*, there is an adverb clause *when you get to the top of the hill* which really refers to place, i.e. at the top of the hill, rather than to time, i.e. the arrival time at the top of the hill. This applies particularly in examples such as this one where directions are given in terms of a person's movements from one place to another which involve both place and time.

Adverb clauses of reason, purpose and result may be taken together, for they all imply some causal relationship between the main and the subordinate clause. Reason clauses are introduced by conjunctions such as *because* or *since*, and purpose and result clauses by *that*, though in the former case *that* implies *in order that* and in the latter *with the result that*. Result clauses usually have an intensifier adverb such as *so* or pre-determiner such as *such* in the main clause. Consider the following examples:

1 Because he had written fifteen books he was made a professor.
2 He wrote fifteen books so that they would make him a professor.
3 He wrote so many books that they made him a professor.

Sentence 1 is a reason clause in which the subordinate adverb clause indicates the reason which causes the action of the main clause. The reason is *because he had written fifteen books*, and this causes the main clause *he was made a professor*. The main clause is the result of the subordinate. The reverse of this is found in sentence 3. Here the result is expressed in the subordinate adverb clause *that they made him a professor*. The main clause is *he wrote so many books*, in which there is an intensifier *so*. The result clause is introduced by *that*, which can be understood as indicating *with the result that*. Both these sentences express a cause and a result, and they differ in that in one the cause is in the subordinate clause and the result in the main clause, and in the other these positions are reversed. Sentence 2 contains a purpose adverb clause. In this type of sentence an action is undertaken in order to produce a result, though it may not be clear whether the result actually happened or not. In sentence 2 there is no indication that the person was made a professor; the implication is only that he undertook a certain action, i.e. writing fifteen books, in the expectation of producing a particular result, i.e. being made a professor. In modern English the uncertainty of the result following the action is often indicated through the use of an auxiliary such as *would*; in earlier English it was expressed through the subjunctive. However, in order to avoid the use of auxiliaries it has become increasingly common in modern English to express purpose through a non-finite adverb clause, in particular through the use of the non-finite infinitive form. Sentence 2 might more characteristically be expressed as *He wrote fifteen books to be made a professor*. When purpose is expressed in this way there is a greater sense that the desired goal was in fact achieved. The action which is undertaken for a purpose is put in the main clause and the result which one hopes will follow is put in the subordinate adverb clause. Adverb clauses of reason may be put either before or after the main clause they refer to, but adverb clauses of purpose or result are almost invariably put after the main clause. Sentence 1 could readily be rewritten *He was made a professor because he wrote fifteen books*, but sentences 2 and 3 could not be rewritten by putting the adverb clause first. When purpose is expressed through a non-finite adverb clause, it is possible to put the infinitive before the main clause as in *To be made a professor he wrote fifteen books*, though this order is considered somewhat literary.

The other types of adverb clause are those of condition, concession and contrast. Conditional adverb clauses are frequently introduced by *if*, though they may be introduced by other conjunctions such as *unless* or *on condition that*. The most common type of conditional clause is that which expresses a condition which has to be fulfilled in order to allow the statement in the main clause to become operative. In *If Dorinda comes home on time, we'll all go to the theatre*, the conditional clause is *if Dorinda comes home on time*. This clause expresses a condition which if it is fulfilled will lead to the fulfilment of the statement in the main clause, i.e. that we will all go to the theatre. The statement can be expressed more negatively through the use of *unless* to introduce the conditional clause, and the occurrence of *not* or *no* in the main clause. This would then produce something like *Unless Dorinda comes home on time, there will be no visit to the theatre*. The examples used so far indicate realistic conditions and plausible statements. But conditional clauses may also be used rhetorically to express some condition which the speaker regards as quite unrealistic, and hence the main clause indicates some statement which is patently false because the condition will never be realised. In *If Dorinda comes home on time tonight, I'm a Dutchman* it is implied that there is no realistic possibility that she will come home on time, for both speaker and listener understand that the speaker is not a Dutchman and could not be suddenly transformed into one. Traditionally the verbs in conditional clauses were put into the subjunctive and remains of this usage may still be found in such expressions as *If I were you* .... They may also occur in legal documents and more formal varieties of language. In colloquial and less formal varieties the subjunctive form is replaced by the appropriate indicative form or by the auxiliary *should* with the base form.

Concessive clauses are introduced by *though, even if* and similar conjunctions. Sentences with concessive clauses indicate that the state of affairs which is indicated by the main clause is contrary to what might have been expected from the information provided in the concessive clause. In the sentence *Although her father is a millionaire she is not happy*, the concessive clause is *Although her father is a millionaire*. The main clause *she is not happy* indicates a state of affairs which is contrary to what might have been expected – namely, that anyone who has a millionaire as a father could be expected to be happy. Concessive clauses may refer to present time or to future time, and those which refer to the future contain an element of uncertainty as to their actual occurrence and so approximate closely to conditional clauses. In such cases *though* and *if* are often interchangeable. The verb in the concessive clause may take the subjunctive form when the reference is to future time: *Though he arrive late, we will still have to go*, but such forms are becoming increasingly rare.

Clauses of condition and of concession may be formed without an introductory conjunction. In these cases there is inversion of the subject and predicator (or more usually the auxiliary part of the verb group acting as predicator). When this happens it may sometimes be difficult to decide whether the clause is one of condition or concession. In *Should he arrive late, we will still have to go* the adverb clause is *Should he arrive late*, which has no introductory conjunction and has the auxiliary *should* before the subject *he*. This adverb clause is best interpreted as a concessive clause meaning 'Though he arrive late', though it might be possible to understand it as a conditional clause meaning 'If he arrives late'. These two adverb clauses are also frequently subject to ellipsis. If the subject of the main and the subordinate clauses is the same, then the subject and predicator of the subordinate clause may be omitted. In *Though late, we will still have to go to the dinner* there is an elliptical concessive clause *though late*, which stands for *though we are late*. The subject *we* of the main clause is understood to apply to the adverb clause too. But even if the subject is not identical it may be omitted in the subordinate clause, particularly if the subject is understood to be an impersonal one such as *it*. Hence in the sentence *if possible we'll come early* there is an elliptical conditional clause *if possible* standing for *If it is possible*.

Adverb clauses of contrast place a statement in contrast with what is indicated in the main clause; they are introduced by some of the same conjunctions used in concessive clauses. In *Mr Smith works in industry, whereas his brother is a teacher* the two clauses contrast the occupations of the brothers. The contrastive clause is *whereas his brother is a teacher*, which acts as a subordinate clause. It would have been possible to express this contrast with a co-ordinating conjunction such as *but*, to give *Mr Smith works in industry, but his brother is a teacher*. In this example each clause is a main clause because *but* is a co-ordinating and not a subordinating conjunction.

Although it is possible to divide adverb clauses into various categories, it may have become clear during the preceding account that the functions of the various clauses overlap and it is consequently difficult to draw a sharp distinction between them in many cases. Some defenders of good English object to the combined *if and when*, an expression which is found quite frequently today as a single conjunction. It is often said that a sentence such as *If and when he comes, we'll go* is clumsy and unnecessarily repetitive, because *if* implies *when* and vice versa. Whether this is so or not, we have to accept that this combined form is now common. It does indicate that speakers of the language are prepared to see time and condition linked in the same clause. Certainly many sentences with an adverb clause of time do indicate a contingency. If on a ship you saw the notice *When you hear three blasts on the ship's siren, proceed immediately to the deck*, you would not assume that you were definitely going to hear three blasts of the ship's siren on your journey; you would understand it to imply the condition 'if you hear three blasts'. So, although the conjunction which introduces an adverb clause will usually provide you with the necessary information as to what type of adverb clause it is, the implication of that clause may be somewhat different from that which clauses of the type normally indicate.

9 Conclusion

This book contains an account of traditional grammar which has been modified by some elements of more modern approaches to language. The result may be a little eclectic since it draws from both traditions, but it should provide the necessary basis for the understanding of many modern grammars except those which are based exclusively on a contemporary theoretical approach such as transformational generative grammar. But most current descriptions of our language presuppose some acquaintance with traditional concepts and also adopt an approach which combines elements of both traditions. This book does not set out to provide a complete account of English; it attempts to give some understanding of a basic methodology of analysing the language together with some insight into the major characteristics of the contemporary language. Since the basis for the analysis provided in this book is written English, it should allow a reader who has mastered the principles involved to apply them to written English of periods other than our own. Since so much of the literature that we read is from previous periods, this clearly is a matter of some importance.

There are three major reasons why someone might want to read a grammar of this sort. The first is to get some understanding of the structure of modern English for its own sake, for teaching purposes, or for comparison with other languages or with earlier varieties of English. At several places in the book I have mentioned changes that have affected the structure of English. For example, today we have only one second person personal pronoun, *you*, whereas in the past we had a singular and a plural form, *thou* and *you*. These two forms were used to distinguish not so much singular and plural as informal and formal levels of discourse, as is true in modern German and French. This means that today in modern English we no longer have a pronominal mechanism for indicating a level of formality and we are consequently forced to adopt a different strategy in our discourse to achieve the same end. This difference is of some importance in appreciating what has survived from past ages. The second is to have some understanding of current usage as a guide to speaking and writing. Books on grammar are not, however, to be confused with books on usage, and those who want to know particular points about what they should or should not write will not have found the solution to their problems here. Yet a knowledge of the structure of the language, the way in which words are built up into groups and these in turn into clauses, may be a help in the composition of English sentences so that they are presented as clearly and as effectively as possible. The third is to acquire a technique for analysing what has been written by others, particularly those works such as literary creations on which it is usually considered worthwhile to spend time and effort to see how they have achieved their effects.

The use to which grammatical information is to be put may dictate the type of analysis to be imposed upon a specific text. There are, however, two basic approaches to analysis. The first is that which merely concerns itself with the classes of words found in the text in question; the second is that which tries to unravel the syntactic structure of the sentences to show how they are organised. Let us take each of these in turn. The division of a text into the individual word classes is what used to be known as parsing and naturally throws into focus the types of word used rather than the way in which they are linked together. The simplest way to do this is by writing in the appropriate word class above each word in the text. If one takes, for example, the relatively simple sentence *The boy who lives round the corner has run away*, it would be possible to set out an analysis in the following way. Every word will have its word class written above it:

article	noun	relative pronoun	verb	preposition
The	boy	who	lives	round

article	noun	auxiliary verb	verb (past participle)	adverb
the	corner	has	run	away.

This type of analysis tells us nothing about the structure of the sentence, for there is no indication as to which word is the subject or about which words are most closely linked in the sentence. Naturally it is possible to superimpose upon this basic analysis a further layer of analysis to reveal which part of the sentence is subject and so on to give something like

SUBJECT

article	noun	relative pronoun	verb	preposition	article	noun
The	boy	who	lives	round	the	corner

PREDICATOR ADJUNCT

auxiliary verb	verb	adverb
has	run	away

But if one is going to this stage it is probably simpler to follow the other type of analysis, which tackles structure as its primary concern.

The analysis which throws word classes into prominence is useful for certain types of investigation. Naturally any investigation which seeks to inquire into the types of word used and what their respective ratios are will rely on this method. As I suggested in the Introduction, it is words which are frequently highlighted in literature, and a great deal of stylistic investigation is consequently based on word-class analysis. Although primary parsing will simply indicate what word classes are employed, it is possible to break down those classes into their constituents so that the word class noun can be broken down into the different types of noun – proper, common, abstract and collective. The extent to which an author uses more of one type may be significant in illustrating how he achieves particular effects.

The analysis which considers structure at a primary level does not start with a word-by-word categorisation, but takes each sentence and breaks it down into its major constituents, and these in turn are broken down into their constituents, and so on. The sentence consists of clauses; clauses are made up of subject, predicator, object, complement and adjunct; these in turn are made up of groups, which are in turn composed of phrases and/or words. An analysis must make clear each of these stages in the break-down of any sentence. Two methods are normally employed to reveal these different levels: the first is the tree diagram and the second the bracketed sentence. The tree diagram works rather like a family tree, which starts with the sentence at the top and breaks down into branches and sub-branches as it descends. If a sentence consists of two clauses this will be shown as

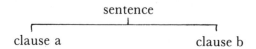

sentence

clause a   clause b

At least one of the clauses will be a main clause. Each clause will in turn have various branches dependent upon it, and this could be represented in the following way

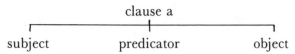

clause a

subject   predicator   object

Each of these sub-branches will in its turn have further branches dependent upon it. The bracketed sentence works on the principle that each structural unit in the sentence is surrounded by a pair of brackets. If one has a sentence with two clauses, one could represent this symbolically as follows:

((clause a)(clause b))

This means that the brackets which enclose the whole represent the sentence; and within those external brackets there are two sets of brackets enclosing clause a and clause b respectively to reveal the constituent parts of the sentence.

The analysis starts with the sentence in each case and can show the composition of the sentence down to word level, though it is possib!e to stop the analysis at any stage on the hierarchical chain. If one wishes only to discuss the use of groups in a particular text, then the analysis will go down only to group level; it will not be necessary to take it down to word level.

There are advantages and disadvantages with each system. These can be more clearly revealed is a simple analysis is undertaken in each method. Let us take the same sentence, *The boy who lives round the corner has run away*, as an example. In a tree diagram this might look roughly as follows:

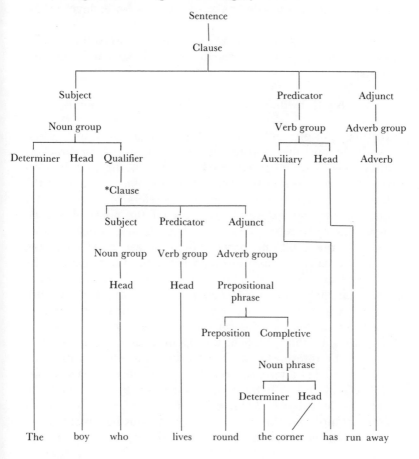

The disadvantage with this system is that it takes up so much space, and where a long text needs to be analysed it would be difficult to carry it out in any concise way. It does reveal each step in the hierarchical chain so that the precise make-up of a sentence is clearly exhibited. The actual words which make up the sentence are not entered till the bottom line, for all the other steps indicate functional aspects of the structure. In the middle of the analysis there is the heading '*Clause', which indicates that there is a clause which is part of a group, in this case a noun group. The asterisk indicates its subordinate status, in so far as it does not function as a clause at what is the true clause level, immediately underneath the sentence; it operates as a clause at a lower level in the hierarchy.

The same sentence, if it were analysed in accordance with the bracketed sentence system, might look something like this:

(((The)(boy)((who)(lives)((round)((the)(corner)))))((has)(run))(away))

In this example each closing bracket refers back to the first available opening bracket. Thus the five closing brackets after *corner* can be interpreted as follows: the first bracket refers to the opening bracket in front of *corner* to mark off the head of the noun phrase; the second refers back to the first opening bracket before *the* to mark off the noun phrase *the corner*; the third refers back to the first opening bracket before *round* to mark off the prepositional phrase *round the corner*, which is acting as an adjunct in the subordinate clause; the fourth refers back to the first opening bracket in front of *who* to mark off the qualifier *who lives round the corner*; and the fifth refers back to the second opening bracket in front of *The* to mark off the subject *The boy who lives round the corner*. At the beginning of the sentence, the opening brackets in front of *The* can be interpreted as follows: the first refers to the final closing bracket after *away* to indicate the sentence as a whole; the second refers to the final closing bracket after *corner* to indicate the subject *The boy who lives round the corner*, which is a noun group; and the third refers to the closing bracket after *The* which indicates the determiner *The* in that noun group.

This type of analysis takes up much less room than the tree diagram, but with complicated structures the number of brackets can grow so large as to be more confusing than illuminating. Furthermore, although the brackets reveal the structure of the sentence, they do not explain the structure, because each step in the sentence hierarchy is not labelled as it is in the tree diagram. For those who are very familiar with sentence analysis, this will present no problem, but for those just embarking on it this could well be a drawback. Probably brackets are useful when only the basic structure, such as clauses, is being illuminated, and tree diagrams should be employed when a sentence structure has to be analysed in greater depth. The indication of word classes is useful when the vocabulary is being examined.

What remains important is the ability to do the necessary analysis on any sentence that needs to be discussed in detail. After a time familiarity should enable any user to point to those parts in a text which are significant without going through the whole process of analysing every sentence down to its particular word classes. The purpose for which the analysis is made will dictate the depth of analysis and the particular methodology chosen. I hope that what has been provided in this book will enable its readers to make that choice in an informed way and to give them the confidence to carry out whatever analysis they think necessary to illustrate the point which need to be highlighted in the text they have chosen to discuss.

Suggested Further Reading

The most complete grammar of English is Randolph Quirk *et al.*, *A Comprehensive Grammar of the English Language* (London: Longman, 1985). A shorter version of it is R. Quirk and S. Greenbaum, *A University Grammar of English* (London: Longman, 1973). For a brief modern grammar there is Geoffrey Leech, Margaret Deuchar and Robert Hoogenraad, *English Grammar for Today, A New Introduction* (London: Macmillan, 1982). For a brief and traditional survey of syntax there is C. T. Onions, revised by B. D. H. Miller, *Modern English Syntax* (London: Routledge and Kegan Paul, 1971). M. A. K. Halliday's *An Introduction to Functional Grammar* (London: Arnold, 1985) presents a full introduction to modern approaches to grammar.

The most complete dictionary of English is J. A. H. Murray *et al.*, *The Oxford English Dictionary* (Oxford: Clarendon Press, 1933), with supplementary volumes edited by R. W. Burchfield (1972–86). There are many shorter and more up-to-date dictionaries; a convenient one is *Collins Dictionary of the English Language*, edicted by P. Hanks. Second edition (London and Glasgow: Collins, 1986).

For general surveys of modern linguistics David Crystal's *What is Linguistics?*, 4th edition (London: Arnold, 1985), presents a brief introduction, while John Lyons's *Introduction to Theoretical Linguistics* (Cambridge: Cambridge University Press, 1968) contains a fuller and more academic account. For a brief account of different approaches to language see George Yule, *The Study of Language: An Introduction* (Cambridge: Cambridge University Press, 1985).

Other aspects of language are covered by G. V. Carey, *Mind the Stop: A Brief Guide to Punctuation* (Cambridge:

Cambridge University Press, 1939; Harmondsworth: Penguin Books, 1976); W. R. O'Donnell and Loreto Todd, *Variety in Contemporary English* (London: George Allen and Unwin, 1980); Barbara M. H. Strang, *A History of English* (London: Methuen, 1970); R. W. Burchfield, *The English Language* (Oxford: Oxford University Press, 1985); and James and Lesley Milroy, *Authority in Language: Investigating Language Prescription and Standardisation* (London: Routledge and Kegan Paul, 1985).

There are numerous books on usage in English. A review of some of the major controversies regarding usage is provided in David Crystal, *Who Cares about English Usage?* (Harmondsworth: Penguin Books, 1984).

Index